Copyright © 1994 by David R. Ord and Robert B. Coote
Published by Orbis Books, Maryknoll, NY 10545
All rights reserved
Manufactured in the United States of America

Library of Congress Cataloging-in-Publication Data

Ord, David Robert.
    Is the Bible true? : making sense of the Bible today / David
Robert Ord and Robert B. Coote.
        p. cm.
    Includes bibliographical references.
    ISBN 0-88344-948-X
    1. Bible — Evidences, authority, etc. 2. Bible — Sources. 3. J
document (Biblical criticism) I. Coote, Robert B., 1944-
II. Title.
BS480.0736   1994
220.1 — dc20   93-37570
                                               CIP

Contents

Preface

This is the third book on which the authors, one a minister and writer, the other a biblical historian, have collaborated. The first, *The Bible's First History,* was published in 1989, and the second, *In the Beginning,* in 1992. They take their place among thousands of other books which make a detailed study of aspects of the Bible.

The current work is different. It is written specifically for the lay person. It seeks to place in the hands of the reader vital information about the Bible that would perhaps not otherwise easily be accessible. It introduces the reader to a way of reading the Bible known to scholars for a very long time, but not often brought to the attention of the lay person.

The authors are indebted to countless scholars for the information presented in this book. How can one acknowledge all the many books, teachers, and colleagues who have contributed to one's understanding? The concept of the Bible as a work meaningful for the twenty-first century that is set forth in this book is a condensing of many years of exposure to the earnest efforts of so many who have struggled to understand the Bible.

We are indebted in particular, however, to Dr. Herman C. Waetjen, Robert S. Dollar Professor of New Testament at San Francisco Theological Seminary. We are especially grateful for the insights that led to the interpretation of the second chapter of the Gospel of John, presented as an example of the new way of reading Scripture suggested in this book.

The authors are also indebted to Robert Ellsberg, Editor in Chief of Orbis Books, for a great many editorial suggestions that prompted a reworking of the original manuscript into what we believe is a much more readable form. We are also grateful for his enthusiasm for this project.

Part One addresses the question of how the Bible should be read. It traces the experience of a person who has grown up reading the Bible literally, but who on closer inspection discovers that what was thought to be "taking the Bible literally" was in reality not literal enough. A study of Scripture ensues, leading to a new approach to reading the Bible.

Part Two asks the question of how the Bible came into being. The Old and New Testaments were produced over a span of a thousand years or more. Who began the writing process, and how were the books collected into their present form? Exactly what is the Bible?

Part Three is about reading the Bible in a way that is meaningful for our lives as we enter the third millennium since the founding of the church. What does it mean to speak of the Bible as "inspired"? How can the Bible be of help to us in sorting out the difficult issues that confront us in our technological era?

A note about the use of the terms "Jew" and "Judean." Translating biblical terms into modern English is no easy task. One of the difficulties is that words change meaning over a period of centuries. Consider the word "America." Are we speaking of North America, Central America, South America, or all three? Or perhaps we are speaking of the political entity known as the United States? It depends on who uses the word, the context in which it is used, and the time period spoken of. When Columbus first came to the shores of North America, the word America had a very different meaning from its popular use today as a way of speaking of the United States. Until only a few decades ago, to speak of America did not conjure up visions of skyscrapers, freeways, the White House, Hollywood, or McDonald's—and for many people elsewhere in the Americas, it still doesn't. Even though the word is the same word that was in existence long ago, what the word connotes has changed drastically.

The same is true of the biblical term frequently translated "Jew." To speak of the Jews today is not the same as to speak of the people of Judea during the centuries immediately before and after the time of Jesus. The religion of the people who lived in this period should be referred to as Judean religion, and the people who practiced this religion should be referred to as

Judeans, even if they lived beyond the boundaries of Judea. In this book we follow the scholarly trend of referring to the people and the religion in this way.

Christianity had its roots in Judean religion. Judaism, the religion of the Jews, also had its roots in Judean religion. Both, however, developed in quite different directions. Judaism is the religion of the rabbis, centered in the synagogue and Talmud instead of the temple, and it flourished after the destruction of the temple in Jerusalem in 70 C.E. It is not to be confused with the term "Jew" as used in the gospels, which ought to be translated "Judean" for greater clarity. The term Judean embraces a wide variety of peoples, only some of whom became the modern Jews. To suggest that it was modern Judaism that crucified Jesus, the "King of the Judeans," is in error. A failure to note this difference has contributed to anti-Semitism down through the centuries.

While the authors worked on this book, their families many times were asked to exercise patience. Appreciation goes to Julian Ord, who many times waited patiently while his father completed a section of the manuscript. Gratitude is also due Margaret Coote for sharing her father's enthusiasm for writing, to Marian Coote, for her careful reading, and to Polly Coote, whose cheerful encouragement spurred on her husband's efforts.

Introduction

What This Book Is About

To ask whether the Bible is "true" brings us face to face with the question Pontius Pilate asked of Jesus on trial for his life: "What is truth?"

Truth, for millions who claim to be Christians, is found in the Bible. A heritage of both the Protestant and Catholic reformations has been an emphasis on the centrality of Scripture and the right of all of us to read the Bible for ourselves. Today both Protestants and Catholics engage in personal Bible study and utilize Scripture as a guide for conduct. But along with the blessings that come from reading Scripture, this heritage has spawned a maze of conflicting individualistic interpretations, all of them claiming to be the truth.

How conflicting these interpretations can be, and how they affect even the most intimate aspects of our lives, can be seen in the case of a Wesleyan minister who made national headlines when he refused to perform a marriage ceremony. A week before the wedding was to take place, he discovered that the fiancé of the young lady whose marriage he was to perform was black. The minister claimed that the Bible forbids interracial marriage. Another minister had no problem marrying the couple. Whose interpretation was right? Is it simply a matter of each of us discerning what the Bible says for ourselves? Or is there a more objective way of approaching Scripture?

To read the Bible is to encounter a world very different from our own. However one understands inspiration, when all is said and done the Bible was written down by scribes who lived at a certain moment in history and in a particular culture. In this book we affirm that to understand what is being said we must know something of how those who put stylus to parchment and papyrus thought. We believe that purely personal interpretation of the Bible from the viewpoint of our modern culture will inevitably miss the mark when it comes to capturing the full richness of God's revelation through these ancient writers. What modern people *think* the Bible says is secondary to *what its writers thought they were saying.*

One aim of this book is to introduce the reader to tools developed by scholars to help throw light on the meanings of the original authors of Scripture. Through the efforts of historians and linguists over the last few hundred years, and especially in recent decades, it has become possible to "get in touch" with the civilizations in which the Bible arose. Today we can know far more of the mind-set of the peoples of biblical times than has been possible at any time since the close of the period of biblical revelation. Understanding something of how the biblical authors thought will inevitably steer the reader away from distorted individualistic interpretations of Scripture, enabling the Word of God as the authors understood it to be heard more accurately.

A second aim of this book is to help the churches struggle with the key issues that occupy Catholics, Protestants, and Orthodox alike as they seek to witness to Christ in modern society. In offering such help, we will not attempt to answer specific questions with which the spiritual community is wrestling. Not only is it beyond the scope of this book to treat issues of moral or ecclesiastical import; to assume that these questions can be decided by a simplistic appeal to a "thus saith the Lord" in Scripture is to fail to understand the purpose of Scripture. Our help is offered in an indirect manner. Aware that the deep divisions that exist between the many branches of Christendom are largely based upon or expressed through differences in the interpretation of the Bible, we seek to present Scripture in a way that may furnish a broader base for discussion.

For instance, in 1992 by a narrow vote the bishops of the Church of England overturned a tradition of almost two thousand years that only males could be admitted to the priesthood. So significant was the vote that it abruptly arrested the movement toward reconciliation of the Church of England and the Church of Rome. At the heart of the debate was interpretation of Scripture. In the Roman tradition — and for many in the Anglican community, not to mention the Orthodox churches and large Protestant bodies such as a majority of Southern Baptists — the selection of twelve males to spread the gospel is understood literally and therefore definitively: women cannot be ordained. Even Catholics are in disagreement over the interpretation of Scripture on the issue of ordination, with many (especially in North America) insisting that women should be allowed into the priesthood.

It is not only on ecclesiastical issues that the churches are divided in their understanding of the truth of Scripture, but also on international issues. The South African conflict is seen from entirely different viewpoints by equally sincere believers. For some it has been a matter of conscience that seminaries and governing bodies divest themselves of investments in South Africa. For others, supporting the South African economy by maintaining investments is viewed as the best way to help the oppressed. Both sides appeal to Scripture to support their views. In the Gulf War, some Christians took a public stand with the Allied forces, while others decried the use of military force. Both groups supported their stand from the Bible. Everywhere we look, committed Christians of different denominational hues reach conflicting conclusions on central questions of the faith based on their reading of the Bible and the sense in which they understand it to be true.

Different views on moral issues are also rooted in how various peoples read the Bible. Pronouncements by church groups attempting to influence public policy on moral issues are in the headlines frequently. Within hours of taking office, President Clinton set the United States aflame over two key moral issues: gays in the military, and the right of a woman to terminate a pregnancy. White House and Congressional phone lines were jammed on the gay rights issue, with many of the protesters basing their objections to the President's decision on a reading of Scripture. For some, statements in the Old Testament and by the apostle Paul condemn homosexuality outright. Others interpret these statements in a quite different light. Meanwhile, across America abortion clinics are besieged by opponents of abortion, some of whom have been jailed for the manner of their protests. Tens of thousands demonstrate. The Bible, many claim, does not allow the taking of the life of a fetus, while others equally committed to a faith position argue that the Bible does not rule out abortion.

What the Bible says about human sexuality is one of the hottest topics of the decade for the churches. Presbyterians, Episcopalians, Methodists, members of the United Church of Christ, and Lutherans are among those who have debated or are in process of debating the issue. Among Catholics there is growing pressure to permit priests to marry. The United Church of Christ already ordains homosexuals. Left and right factions of the Episcopal Church in its 1991 convocation both sought a definitive statement not only on homosexuality but also on the whole issue of human sexuality; instead, the denomination recommended that the church restudy the issues. Meanwhile a United Methodist study committee has indicated its opposition to that church's traditional stance that homosexual practice is incompatible with Christianity.

The Presbyterian Church's *Human Sexuality* report highlights the clash of opinion in America today concerning the relevance of the Bible. A committee member who opposed the report got to the heart of the issue when he stated that the report "gives the appearance to people that they just *threw the Bible out.*" Christians from many churches became embroiled in the battle, many of them chanting outside the denomination's annual assembly, "Don't compromise the Word of God." With its overwhelming vote to reject the report, the Assembly declared in a pastoral letter, "We have reaffirmed in no uncertain terms *the authority of the scriptures* of the Old and New Testaments."

It is our intention in this book to help make the Bible practical for the world of the twenty-first century. How we read the Bible makes all the difference to our day-to-day faith. The question of gays, and of abortion, is not only a question of church policy: these are highly personal issues. If a Christian discovers a gay orientation, how does faith impact that orientation? If a teenager becomes pregnant, is abortion a responsible act or out of the question? And what of the traditional moral values said to be upheld by the Bible: is sex outside of marriage always wrong? Is divorce permissible under any and all circumstances, and may divorced people remarry? These biblical issues touch the heart and soul of our daily lives.

Since the Bible is the church's primary resource for addressing these and the myriad other issues that people want answers on, it will be helpful to have an overview of the contents and development of the Bible. This we shall attempt to furnish. Many who claim to believe the Bible in many cases do not know precisely what the Bible says on a particular issue. The conflict over the "truth" of the biblical creation story is a case in point. States battle over the teaching in public schools of the evolution of the universe and particularly the human species. Some seek to mandate that the biblical creation story be taught alongside evolution. Others argue that the biblical creation account is irrelevant in our modern scientific era. Across the nation, textbooks are rewritten at great expense to lessen the offence of evolution to creationists. But in all of the controversy, perhaps the question that needs to be asked is: "Is there a single, definitive creation story in the Bible?" It is a thesis of this book that when we have a clearer understanding of the content of Scripture and of how it was put together, we shall see more clearly in what sense the Bible may be said to be true.

All of this is to say that it is possible for people to affirm the "truth" of Scripture and mean very different things. For one person it is essential that every event described in the Bible happened exactly as depicted, or the Bible is not true. For another the Bible can be the Word of God even if it is not always historically accurate, and even if there are issues on which he or she thinks differently. One feels that to believe the Bible is true means taking every word of Scripture literally. Another claims to believe the Bible yet does not for one moment imagine that the original authors, Jesus, or the church that canonized Scripture intended it to be thought of as either factual or binding on all peoples for all time.

In answering the question of the truth of the Bible, a central issue is whether we equate truth with fact. In our society there are many for whom something cannot be true if it is not factual. But what of the writers of the ancient world by whose pens the many books that make up the Bible were composed? Did they understand truth to be conveyed only through factual statements? This is the bedrock issue this book grapples with.

The question of *what the Bible says* and in *what sense what it says is true* is indeed the question for today's church. And not only for the church. Millions in Western society no longer affiliate with organized religion yet long for spirituality. While unable to accept traditional views of the Bible, they remain open to be influenced by the book upon which not only Judaism and Christianity are founded but which has also been the basis of much of Western civilization.

It is for those both within and outside of the church who want to know whether the Bible is true that this book is written. The book is the product of collaboration between a minister and a biblical scholar. It is not our intention to furnish answers to the question of what the Bible says on specific issues. Neither interracial marriage, abortion, the origin of the universe, nor human sexuality are our topic. Rather our objective is to enable anyone with interest in the Bible to discover what the Bible says and to evaluate in what sense the Bible is true. It is our hope that church and society in the twenty-first century will discover a fruitful way of reading the book that has for generations been the world's best seller, enabling all of us to hear the Word of God in Scripture afresh.

Part 1

IS THE BIBLE TRUE?

1.

Will the Real Santa Please
Stand Up

It was November. The leaves of the trees were turning many shades of gold, red, and brown, and although the days were still warm and sunny, there was a chill in the air at night now. To a little boy the approach of winter spelled Christmas.

Already stores were stocking shelves with seasonal gifts and decorations, the airwaves vibrated with messages about what was new in gifts this year, and it was about a month since the little boy and his father bought several pounds of dried fruit and baked their Christmas cake.

The youngster knew well in advance what he wanted from Santa that year: "A choo choo train!" And he would have one, for when his father was small like him, he had received from his father his first electric HO gauge locomotive. The young lad would have his electric "choo choo train" because that very locomotive rested in a hidden box in their home waiting for Christmas when the father would pass it on.

That locomotive, together with other locomotives and rolling stock, came into the family's possession via the Christmas stocking from year to year. It was the custom on Christmas Eve, several hours after their son had retired for the night, for the parents to busy themselves stuffing boxes of all shapes and sizes into pillow cases, finally hauling them to rest at the foot of the little boy's bed.

When Christmas morning finally dawned and he dragged his "sack," as he called it, into mom and dad's bed to open the gifts, careful note was taken of the colorful little tag attached to each package. There was Aunt Becky to thank for a diesel engine, Uncle Fred to write in appreciation for a new station, and Aunt Edith to kiss for the new railway carriage. Santa had been most generous once again.

In all of those boyhood years of believing in Santa Claus, it never occurred to the little boy that there was a discrepancy over the source of the gifts. He asked Santa for them months in advance, and until he was about eight he believed Santa brought them; yet he also knew that each of them came from aunts and uncles. It simply never dawned upon his child's mind that gifts could not have come from the North Pole at the same time as from relatives in different parts of the country. Of course, when he grew up he learned that Santa is a mythical figure representing the generosity within people. But as Christmas rolled around once more he was reminded through his own preschooler of those uncomplicated childhood days when both Santa *and* relatives were the simultaneous source of his delight.

Even as he grew up with an implicit belief in Santa Claus, so also he grew up with an implicit belief in the Bible. He had been weaned on the Bible. Early in childhood he began singing in the choir at church and attending Sunday school. The older he grew, the more his interest in the Bible developed. As a teenager he had a pretty good knowledge of Scripture. He especially prided himself that he took the Bible literally. He simply read what seemed clear enough to him and believed it.

His Sunday school teachers had drilled into him that the Bible was the manual God bequeathed to humanity to show us the meaning of life and to tell us how to live. This was no mere human book. It was the Word of God, delivered gift-wrapped directly from heaven. No matter what problem confronted him, God had provided through this handbook either a direct solution to his problem or principles that could be applied to it. In a world of uncertainty the Bible offered answers; in times of turmoil it afforded a sense of security.

His trust in the Bible was implicit because he considered it God-breathed and therefore inerrant. This didn't mean there might not be minor scribal errors resulting from textual transmission through the centuries; but he imagined these were readily weeded out: the pure, unadulterated Word of God was still available, despite the fact that only the original manuscripts were actually perfect. The sixty-six books of the Bible formed a beautiful tapestry in which every thread fit.

Not that he wasn't aware there are differences in the way the gospels report the events in Jesus' life. He had a vague idea that there were differences, but he thought no more seriously about them than he did about how both Santa and his relatives could have been the source of his Christmas gifts when he was young. Surely these alleged discrepancies were simply a matter of each evangelist reporting different details. There were books that harmonized the supposedly inharmonious accounts, and it seemed that the differences could be likened to two people taking a ride on a bus and describing what they observed through windows on opposite sides of the bus. Anyway, witnesses rarely describe the same event identically.

In his teenage years he was a diligent Bible student. His wasn't the five minute night cap routine. He studied at least an hour, often several, every day. He felt he really knew the Bible. If someone quoted a passage to him, he could tell them where it was. Scripture was his pride and joy.

It was during a study period that, quite out of the blue, he stumbled across differences between the itinerary of Jesus' ministry as recorded by Mark and John—differences that the bus journey theory seemed unable to account for. Apparently these differences could not be explained in terms of how those responsible for the accounts remembered the events. The crisis of faith this precipitated was as traumatic as discovering that it was relatives who furnished Christmas gifts, not a jolly fat man at the North Pole.

2.

The Differences Are Real

For millions who read Scripture devotionally, the Bible is a seamless garment. This is especially true of the gospels that form the heart and core of the Christian message. They imagine that each gospel adds to the others, and that by taking the gospels as a whole we discover the story of Jesus' life. In other words, the gospels say essentially the same thing: they confirm and add to each other.

It simply never occurs to someone brought up with the belief that the Bible is all of a piece that the gospels in many ways tell quite different stories. Not only can these stories not be reconciled, they were not *meant* to be lumped together as if they were all saying the same thing. The authors intended the differences.

The thing furthest from most people's minds as they ponder their daily devotional would be to contrast the events surrounding the start of Jesus' career as reported by the author of Mark and the author of John. Few notice that there are any differences, and fewer still take the differences seriously. It comes as a shock to faith to realize that the differences are real.

Going in Two Directions at Once

Mark and John both send Jesus on a journey. The problem is that they have him going in two different directions at once.

6

Mark's story opens with John the Baptizer calling folk to repentance and baptizing them in the river Jordan. In addition to baptizing, John announced that one would come after him who would baptize people with the Holy Spirit. The story line continues:

> In those days Jesus came from Nazareth of Galilee and was baptized by John in the Jordan ... The Spirit *immediately* drove him out into the wilderness. *And he was in the wilderness forty days* ... (these and subsequent italics added)

In Mark we learn that immediately following his baptism Jesus went into the wilderness, where he spent forty days. Mark makes it clear that Jesus did not begin preaching or call any disciples until after those forty days of temptation alone in the wilderness were complete.

The story line of John's Gospel is drastically different. John 1:19 records a visit by officials from Jerusalem to inquire concerning John the Baptizer's authority to baptize. Verse 29 reports that "the next day" Jesus himself came to be baptized. (The author is quite specific about the timing of these events, charting the days one by one.) In verse 35 we encounter another time indicator: it was "on the next day"—the day after Jesus' baptism—that Jesus called Andrew and another of John's converts to become his disciples, following which Andrew sought out his brother Simon. Then Jesus and his disciples journeyed to Cana of Galilee where "on the third day" there was a marriage to which they were invited.

In Mark's Gospel the first of the disciples were not called until after Jesus had spent forty days in the wilderness. When John says Jesus was in Cana at a wedding with his disciples, Mark says he was in the wilderness alone and had not even called his disciples yet. Mark says that it was only after the period of temptation that Jesus came into Galilee preaching the gospel. And it was after the forty days, and after he had begun preaching, that he called his first disciples. Whereas in John they had gone with him to the wedding in Cana within two or three days of his baptism, Mark is explicit that they were not with him at all for over forty days after his baptism:

> In those days Jesus came from Nazareth of Galilee and was baptized by John in the Jordan ... The Spirit imme- diately drove him out into the wilderness. And he was *in the wilderness forty days* ... Now after John was arrested, Jesus came into Galilee, preaching the gospel of God ... And passing along by the Sea of Galilee, he saw Simon and Andrew the brother of Simon ... And going on a little farther, he saw James the son of Zebedee and John his brother ...

There is another major difference between Mark and John concerning the timing of the start of Jesus' ministry. This dif- ference has to do with the imprisonment of John the Baptizer. Mark states explicitly:

> Now *after John was arrested,* Jesus came into Galilee, preaching the gospel of God, and saying, "The time is fulfilled, and the kingdom of God is at hand; repent, and believe in the gospel."

According to Mark 1:14, it was *only after John the Baptizer was put in prison* that Jesus came into Galilee proclaiming the good news. Then, after this, he saw Andrew and Simon and called them to follow him. A little later he encountered James and John, calling them too. In contrast, John 3:22-26 states specifi- cally that the calling of the disciples occurred before John the Baptist was imprisoned. Indeed, Jesus and his disciples were baptizing in the land of Judea at the same time that John was still baptizing, in flat disagreement with Mark's account that Jesus did not call his disciples until after John's ministry had concluded. John is specific:

> After this Jesus and his disciples went into the land of Judea; there he remained with them and baptized. *John also was baptizing* at Aenon near Salim, because there was

much water there; and people came and were baptized. For *John had not yet been put in prison.*

The differences continue as we trace the story line of each gospel. After his baptism, forty days in the wilderness, the imprisonment of John, and the calling of his first disciples, Mark tells us that the group journeyed to Capernaum (1:21) where Jesus performed his first mighty deed, the healing of a man with an unclean spirit, in the synagogue. Immediately upon leaving the synagogue they went to the home of Simon and Andrew where Simon's mother-in-law was healed of a fever, also on the Sabbath. Early Sunday morning, Jesus went off to a solitary place to pray, following which he and his party left Capernaum to travel to other villages in Galilee. Mark 2:1 records that it was a few days later that they returned to Capernaum.

John insists that John the Baptizer had not yet been put in prison when Jesus began to preach and call his disciples. John also rules out any period of forty days in the wilderness. And instead of going to Capernaum, John has Jesus and his disciples journey to Cana. There is no getting around John's explicit statements on the timing of events:

Now they had been sent from the Pharisees. They asked him [John the Baptizer], "Then why are you baptizing, if you are neither the Christ, nor Elijah, nor the prophet?" ... *The next day* he saw Jesus coming toward him, and said, "Behold, the Lamb of God, who takes away the sin of the world!" ... And John bore witness, "I saw the Spirit descend as a dove from heaven, and it remained on him ..." *The next day* again John was standing with two of his disciples; and he looked at Jesus as he walked, and said, "Behold, the Lamb of God!" The two disciples heard him say this, and they followed Jesus ... *The next day* Jesus decided to go to Galilee. And he found Philip and said to him, "Follow me." ... *On the third day* there was a marriage at Cana in Galilee, and the mother of Jesus was there; Jesus also was invited to the marriage, with his disciples.

In John's Gospel it was the very next day after the calling of the two sets of brothers that the party left for Galilee. Chapter two opens with the statement that they then attended the marriage in Cana of Galilee, where Jesus turned water into wine (which the evangelist identifies in verse 11 as the very first of Jesus' signs). Only after this does Jesus journey to Capernaum. Following the visit to Capernaum he leaves to observe the feast of the Passover in Jerusalem.

Most of us have read these accounts time and again without ever noticing how great are the differences between them. Once one actually begins to catalog the anomalies, dismissing them by likening them to people recollecting different aspects of the same events becomes impossible. It is not aspects of events that are reported differently: the events themselves are different.

Who's Telling the Truth?

Let us recap the key differences we have seen so far. When Mark says Jesus was in the wilderness, John has him calling disciples and going to a wedding in Cana. When Mark has him beginning his ministry only after John the Baptizer has finished his ministry, John has the two preaching simultaneously. Both cannot be correct. So who is telling the truth?

The inappropriateness of the analogy of eyewitnesses reporting facts differently may be seen by transporting it into our own century. A husband and wife have been brought in for questioning by the police in connection with a murder. They are interviewed separately. The man states that on the day in question he and his wife were driving from San Francisco to Los Angeles, proceeding the following day to San Diego. His wife, testifying to the same journey, says that they drove from San Francisco to Hearst Castle, where they spent several hours before going on to have dinner in Santa Barbara; then the next morning they visited Marineland of the Pacific, before continuing on for lunch in San Juan Capistrano. It is essential to their defense that their separate accounts corroborate each other; and because they are merely recalling different aspects of the same journey, it is not difficult to harmonize their accounts. That they jibe even though different in detail accords them a certain ring of factuality. They are the same events reported from different angles.

In the gospels, the testimony of the evangelists does not hang together in a harmonious way. It is as if the couple being questioned both insist they were out of town at the time of the murder, but beyond such an assertion they agree on almost nothing. While one describes highlights of Highway 101, including stops at Hearst Castle and Santa Barbara, the other says they took Interstate 5, which misses these places altogether. The only similarity is that at one point they both pass through Los Angeles. Someone's testimony isn't factual! The police rightly become suspicious. It is just such discrepancies that we are faced with in the travelogues of the four gospels.

Nor is it only in the opening events of the gospels that there are major differences. Such differences persist throughout the story line. For instance, Jesus' outrage in the temple appears in a different chronological setting in John's Gospel than in Matthew, Mark, or Luke. This gospel locates it near the beginning of Jesus' ministry, whereas in Mark it takes place in the week leading up to the Passover at the close of his ministry, only days before his execution.

Mark, who catalogues Jesus' ministry with details of the many places he went, makes no allowance for anything other than a single visit to Jerusalem at Passover. Indeed, in Mark this last Passover is the only one Jesus observes in Jerusalem. Jesus begins his ministry in Galilee. He journeys from Galilee to Judea for the first time in Mark 10:1. A period of teaching in Judea interrupts the journey briefly (Mk 10:17). But as Passover approaches, Jesus begins to journey in earnest:

> And they were on the road, going up to Jerusalem, and Jesus was walking ahead of them; and they were amazed, and those who followed were afraid. And taking the twelve again, he began to tell them what was to happen to him, saying, "Behold, we are going up to Jerusalem . . . "

Only at the end of his life does Jesus come to Jerusalem, and the last days of his life occupy the remainder of Mark's Gospel, the eleventh through sixteenth chapters. Here is when Jesus performs an act that results in his crucifixion. This is the most radical act of his entire ministry. On Palm Sunday he rides into Jerusalem, enters the temple and drives out the people and sacrificial animals. Not many days later he is arrested, tried, and crucified.

In John's Gospel, on the other hand, Jesus visits Jerusalem on three occasions, each of them at Passover. In fact, John's Gospel is constructed around three separate Passovers. It is on his first visit to Jerusalem that Jesus ransacks the temple, driving out the animals and expelling the bankers. No such event occurs at either of his succeeding visits.

Not only is the chronology of Jesus' attack upon the temple unique in John's Gospel, but also the context in which the evangelist places the occurrence differs from that of Mark. In the latter it comes on the heels of Jesus' triumphal entry into Jerusalem on Palm Sunday, whereas in John it follows his very first sign, the changing of water into wine at the marriage in Cana of Galilee. And while Mark places after it the cursing of the fig tree, John follows it with a pronouncement by Jesus that left the Jews who heard it utterly bewildered: "Destroy this temple, and in three days I will raise it up" (Jn 2:19). While for Mark this was a culminating act at the end of Jesus' ministry and led to execution, for John it was a definitive act that set the tone for Jesus' ministry that was just beginning.

We have only begun to scratch the surface of the differences in the travelogue of each gospel. It might be an interesting exercise sometime to go through the gospels and actually map out each travelogue in detail, including times, events, and places in order to get an even clearer picture of how divergent they are. What we have here are not two descriptions of the same journey, but two journeys along quite different routes. Clearly the gospels are not a factual account of the life of the historical Jesus.

A Case of a Poor Memory?

A frequent rejoinder when the conflicting testimony of the gospels is pointed out is that they were written many years after the events, with each evangelist collecting whatever stories about Jesus he could either remember or glean from others, stringing them together as best he could. The suggestion is made that John did not know about the forty-day temptation tradition that we read of in Mark, or that he was unaware that Jesus attacked the temple only days before his crucifixion. Not only is this preposterous given the amount of detailed description and dating that John includes, but it is impossible if one holds to the view that these are inerrant writings. One cannot believe in the theory of general recollection and inerrancy at the same time. The idea of inerrancy is that there are no errors because the Bible, in this view, did not originate with fallible humans but with God.

In fact, the countless specific statements in each gospel of when events happened — even including the hour in some instances — preclude viewing these literary works as haphazard, random collections of stories. For instance, it is evident that John has deliberately set Jesus' action in the temple in his own unique context. He placed it at the beginning of his gospel, when he undoubtedly knew full well the tradition from Mark's account (which was in circulation up to a quarter of a century earlier) that it took place at the end of Jesus' ministry. That John was not merely "doing his best to recollect" events is evident from the fact that instead of generalizing he presents us with a precise record of the exact days on which events took place. And how could any author writing "inerrant" Scripture claim that Jesus called his first two disciples "the next day" after his baptism, calling two more disciples "the next day," then "on the third day" attending a wedding in Cana of Galilee, if he either knew from tradition and other gospels that Jesus spent forty days in the wilderness, or had no knowledge of the events whatever and simply made them up to fill out the story? What happens to inerrancy in this case?

Undoubtedly a good deal of woolly thinking persists on this issue because some want to avoid the plain fact that the gospels, if read as factual accounts, flagrantly contradict one another. We are left to ponder in what sense the gospels are "God-breathed." Clearly, inspiration cannot be equated with inerrancy.

3.

In Search of a Christmas Pageant

Although each gospel is essentially different from the others, each is consistent within itself. If the four gospels are not themselves all of a piece, at least within each gospel the message is consistent.

The internal harmony of each gospel suggests that these are not haphazard collections of memories that we are dealing with but narratives which have been deliberately constructed as we find them—constructed that way even though the author was fully aware that what he was writing would differ from other accounts of Jesus' life and ministry.

To pass over these many differences as if they are failures of memory is to do a gross injustice to the extremely detailed nature of each gospel and to miss the author's intent altogether. All attempts to harmonize the gospels actually distort the vital teaching each evangelist sought to convey by deliberately incorporating differences into his narrative. The more closely we study each gospel, the more the conflict between them cries out for acknowledgment. Instead of attempting to maintain a unity between the gospels, in this chapter we shall accede to the demand of each to be considered in its own right.

Each evangelist's objective was truth that we can live by, not a biography of Jesus' life. Since they were concerned with proclaiming a truth that transcends historicity, to ask whose account of the events surrounding the start of Jesus' ministry is factual is to ask a question the authors never intended their readers to put to the text. We must read each gospel not to discover what actually happened but as a portrait in words of the Christ and his meaning for our lives. The historical realities that we might think are supposed to lie behind the accounts of Jesus' birth, life, death, and resurrection, as far as the author thought he knew them, are subordinated by each author in his own unique way to the message he wished to proclaim.

Each gospel seeks to convey an aspect of the Christ that is unique. It is as if the significance of the Christ event were being refracted through a prism, with each author picking up a different color and excluding all the other colors so as to focus our attention on the one.

In order to grasp the messages the evangelists were seeking to convey it will be necessary to enter into the unique story world of each gospel—to live within the author's specially created world. When the gospels were written, they each had a meaning that was contained within their own literary world; originally they were not supposed to go together in what we now call the Bible. It is this independent meaning of each author that we need to dig into if we are to make sense of the gospels. To leap from one story world to another in an effort to piece together an historical reality behind the gospels is to violate the nature of a gospel. To hop from gospel to gospel is to make of the Bible an unintelligible mishmash. This is one reason there is so much disagreement within Christianity over what the Bible says. We must unearth why each author wrote what he wrote by searching for the meaning of an event within the world of that gospel, rather than trying to explain a feature of a particular gospel by jumping into the entirely different story world of another gospel.

Many have been puzzled as to why there are four gospels, especially when they are so repetitive. The answer will emerge as we learn to live within each gospel as an integral literary work, for we shall discover that even when the same story occurs in all of the gospels, it is used by each evangelist to make a quite different point. The emphasis is different. We miss a writer's message entirely if we simply transfer the meaning of a story in one gospel to the same story in another gospel. By living within each gospel, we shall see how the authors tailor the various stories to the particular audiences and issues they wish to address.

How We Got the Christmas Story

Undoubtedly the best-known story in the gospels is the Christmas story. Surprisingly, however, what has come to be known and reenacted each year as the nativity pageant does not exist in Scripture. Mark's Gospel, which is widely accepted as the earliest of the New Testament gospels to have been written, does not contain any information about the birth of Jesus; and John's Gospel, the last to be written, is completely silent about the virgin birth, the manger, the shepherds, and the wise men. Only Matthew and Luke talk about Jesus' infancy, and they present entirely different stories. It is only by piecing these two stories together that what is known as the Christmas story came into being.

Matthew says nothing about the circumstances of Jesus' birth. There is no suggestion that Mary and Joseph lived in Nazareth, no mention of a census requiring them to travel anywhere to be registered, no journey on a donkey, no manger scene, no angels in the sky, no shepherds. As far as Matthew is concerned, Jesus' family came from Bethlehem. Lying five miles south of Jerusalem, Bethlehem was the ancestral town of David where he was anointed king by the prophet Samuel. Matthew is anxious to portray Jesus as the direct descendant of David dwelling in the city of David.

What we do find in Matthew is a family who was from and lived in Bethlehem. A son is born to them in their own house. Magi from the East (Persian Babylonia) see a star and follow it. The magi visit the family of Jesus in their house and offer them gifts. Herod the king, made aware of the birth of a potential rival by the magi, seeks out the infant Jesus. Fearing for the young child's life, Joseph takes his family to Egypt to live. Herod slaughters all the male infants below the age of two in the vicinity of Bethlehem. After the death of Herod, Joseph returns with his family to Palestine. He attempts to go back to Bethlehem but learns that another dangerous king is now on the throne and instead keeps a low profile seeking out a new home in a backwater of Galilee called Nazareth.

Luke tells an entirely different story from Matthew. There is no house in Bethlehem. There is no star. There are no magi. There is no mention of Herod and the slaughter of the innocents. There is no flight to Egypt, no period of exile, no attempt to return to Bethlehem.

It is in Luke, whose genealogy of Jesus even differs from Matthew's, that the family lived in Nazareth and had to journey to Bethlehem. It is in Luke that they find no place in the inn. It is in Luke that angels sing and shepherds visit the manger. And in Luke the family returns directly to Nazareth immediately upon completion of the requirements of the law, forty days after Jesus' birth.

The problem with most people who want to take the Bible literally is that they often do not take it literally enough. Paying close attention to what Scripture actually says reveals that we are dealing with two irreconcilable stories.

This can readily be illustrated in the statements by Matthew and Luke concerning where Jesus came from. Matthew tells us that "Jesus was born in Bethlehem of Judea," and that the family occupied a house there. After the magi departed Joseph had a dream warning him of danger,

> And he rose and took the child and his mother by night, and departed to Egypt, and remained there until the death of Herod . . . But when Herod died . . . he rose and took the child and his mother, and went to the land of Israel. But when he heard that *Archelaus reigned over Judea* in place of his father Herod, *he was afraid to go there,* and being warned in a dream he withdrew to the district of Galilee. And he went and dwelt in a city called Nazareth, that what was spoken by the prophets might be fulfilled, "He shall be called a Nazarene."

Joseph and Mary had never lived in Nazareth before. Matthew says they went there specifically to fulfill a prophecy: they did not go there because that was their home. They were not returning to Nazareth. Quite the contrary, when they came back from Egypt they did not go to Nazareth but wanted to go to Judea, very likely to their home in Bethlehem. It was only when they realized that to return home to Bethlehem was dangerous that they looked for a new home and found Nazareth. They "went and dwelt in a city called Nazareth," somewhere they had never been before.

How different this is from Luke, who has them coming from Nazareth all along. They never occupy a house in Bethlehem. All of Luke's nativity scenes center around the manger. After his birth Jesus is circumcised and named on the eighth day of his life, following which he is brought to the temple in Jerusalem for the ritual of purification. There is no sense of danger, no mention of fleeing by night to Egypt; everything takes place in broad daylight. Then,

> And when they had performed everything according to the law of the Lord, they returned into Galilee, *to their own city,* Nazareth. (Lk 2:39)

For Luke, Joseph and Mary had always lived in Nazareth; it was not a new home for them, as in Matthew. It was not just "a city called Nazareth" that they came across while searching for a home in the wake of being unable to return to Judea.

It is important to remember that the gospels were not originally composed as part of the New Testament. They were separate books, composed for different readerships, and for a time may have circulated in different regions of the eastern Mediterranean. Matthew and Luke were not attempting to supplement each other's story with information of which the other was not aware. Each tells a wholly separate story, portraying the significance of Christ for peoples with quite different interests and concerns.

Biography—Or a Portrait in Words?

The gospels are not biographies of Jesus. They do not attempt to detail his entire life. They are rather depositions that seek to establish that Jesus is the Christ, depositions submitted in faith by committed followers. They are not historical but theological documents, not chronicles of events but testimonies of faith. They are pictures in words of what Jesus' life means.

Each gospel furnishes us with a unique presentation of the Christ that is intended not as biography but as proclamation. We shall use Matthew to illustrate how a gospel read as a distinct story conveys a message tailored for its unique readership.

Like the other gospel writers, Matthew wrote for a Judean readership living in a Gentile world, probably around 80 or 85 C.E., perhaps specifically for a congregation in Antioch of Syria. There was a large Judean population in Antioch and many of them were wealthy business people. They relied for their success largely upon the network of contacts they maintained with other Judeans throughout the dispersion in the Gentile world. After the collapse of the Judean state in 70 C.E. at the hands of the Romans, the Judean religious leadership, including followers of Jesus Christ, sought to reconstitute their Judean identity in many different ways. One interpretation of Matthew's gospel is that the Judean Christians to whom he addresses himself were being pressured to separate from their Gentile brothers and sisters in the church and become part of a more exclusive Jewish community. Not to do so could cost them heavily. It is this problem that Matthew may address in his gospel. It is a direct appeal to Judean Christians to find God in a church that is composed both of Judeans and Gentiles instead of separating themselves.

Because he is preoccupied with meaning, not historical detail, Matthew moves quickly from his simple statement that Jesus was born in Bethlehem to the arrival of the magi and the story of Herod's attempt to slay the infant king. Where did Matthew get this story? From actual events in Jesus' infancy? When the story is read closely and contrasted with Luke, we shall see that there is good reason to believe that he drew it from familiar themes of the Old Testament. Writing to a principally Judean readership, his aim was to depict Jesus as the hope of Israel, and he used motifs from the familiar stories of the Hebrew Bible to say what Jesus meant.

For one born and bred on the Old Testament, as were the urban Judeans of Matthew's time, there is great teaching in the imagery in which Matthew cloaks Jesus' infancy. Let us consider

first the magi. These wise men were from outside the pale of
Israel's faith. They had seen the infant king's star "in the rising"
(as the Greek expresses it). The magi, students of the stars,
interpreted the star as a sign that a king had been born in Judea.
The magi are portrayed following the star until it reached its
zenith in the sky, at which point it stood directly over the house
in which Jesus lived. Whether we can identify such a star in
history is not essential to the story. A star that rose, appeared
over Jerusalem, turned south to Bethlehem, and then came to
rest over a house would have constituted a celestial phenomenon
unique in astronomical history and of great interest to all star-
gazers; but while we might be tempted to point to possible plan-
etary conjunctions as the "star" of Bethlehem, there is no mention in the astronomical records of a star that moved in the
fantastic manner described by Matthew. The point of the story
is not the astronomical data, but the star's meaning.

Who were these magi? Again, whether they were actual per-
sonages is not essential to Matthew's point. What matters for
Matthew's readership is what the magi represent. The imagery
is drawn from the Hebrew Scriptures. The original "magus"
from the East was a prophet named Balaam who was summoned
by the king of Moab to curse Israel as they approached the
Promised Land. Instead of cursing Israel, God caused Balaam
to bless. "There will come a man out of Israel's seed," he said,
"and he will rule many nations, and his kingdom will be
increased. I see him, but not now; I behold him, but not nigh;
a star shall come forth out of Jacob, and a scepter will rise out
of Israel." Historically, the words were spoken of David, who
emerged as the star monarch of Israel. But among Judeans
before the time of Jesus this statement was widely believed to
point to the expected Messiah. No wonder Matthew drew on
the imagery to speak of Jesus! In Matthew's story Herod is the
counterpart of the king of Moab who seeks to have a magus
curse Israel, but the magi foil the evil king's plan in the tradition
of Balaam.

In the first century, magi were spread throughout the Middle
East. The magi represented Persian interests, in contrast to
Rome's, and Herod had been given his throne by the Romans
when they ousted the Persians from Jerusalem at the beginning

of his reign. Magi were known for their ability to interpret the meaning of dreams. They were also astrologers who could read the meaning of the movements of the stars.

In the Old Testament story of Daniel, Nebuchadnezzar king of Babylon had a dream that the magi of his court could not interpret but which Daniel the exiled Judean explained easily. Years later Belshazzar the king saw supernatural handwriting on the palace wall; once again none of the magi could make sense of it, whereas the Judean Daniel revealed its meaning. In Matthew the situation is reversed. The magi, thought of by those who studied Scripture as heathen, pinpoint the significance of the star.

Through the imagery of the magi, Matthew offers us the paradox of pagans representing the enemy of Herod and the Romans receiving spiritual insight from nature, while those who pride themselves in Scripture are so narrow in their understanding of where and how God is at work in the world as to be spiritually blind. Matthew depicts the scribes and priests of Herod's court searching the Scriptures diligently to understand where the Messiah will come from, but unable to recognize a fulfillment that the heathen could see plainly.

The theme is reinforced by an interwoven motif, that of the persecuting King Herod. Whether we are dealing with history is immediately in question. Matthew says that *all Jerusalem* was disturbed by the magi's announcement that a rival king had been born. Is it not strange that, realizing there exists a threat to his throne, Herod makes no effort to follow the magi in their mere five mile journey from Jerusalem to Bethlehem? Word of magi from the East bringing gifts for a royal infant would have spread throughout the region, especially in such a tight-knit society; yet they flee unnoticed, and Herod's soldiers fail to identify which house they visited. Read as history, this makes no sense. But in Matthew's story world their escape is essential to the message.

The sparing of the infant Jesus from a king who slays all infants is reminiscent of the sparing of Moses in the Old Testament story of the basket in the bulrushes. As the Israelites multiplied, the king of Egypt felt threatened and so ordered that every Hebrew baby boy be massacred. Matthew adds a twist to this Hebrew story: instead of the massacre of the Israelite baby boys being at the hand of the Egyptian king, it is the king of Judah who commits this atrocity. And rather than Egypt being the place where the Israelites are endangered and from which they must flee, in a dramatic reversal of the age-old story of the exodus it is to Egypt that Israel's new king flees for safety. Matthew's message that God's presence is no longer recognized by the rulers of old Israel has been hammered home by Matthew's fresh use of some of the most potent imagery of the Hebrew Scriptures.

In the Old Testament the nation of Israel is spoken of figuratively as a virgin. Though Israel had followed other gods and was therefore unfaithful to the god Yahweh, the prophet still saw her prophetically as the virgin Israel (for example, in Amos 5:2). The Old Testament also speaks of Israel collectively as God's son. One such reference, which Matthew refers back to, is in Hosea: "Out of Egypt I called my son" (11:1). Matthew draws a parallel between Israel collectively and Jesus. He is the true Israelite, the pattern for all authentic Israelites. In him is embodied what God meant Israel to be. The wayward Israel has at last fulfilled her role as the virginal bride of Yahweh and given birth to a legitimate heir. In the imagery of Matthew's drama of persecution in Palestine and escape into Egypt, Jesus lives in his own story a reversal of the history of the Israelite people, pointing to a redemption of pagan peoples. One point Matthew is making is clear: just as we don't expect the Israelite king to slay the infants and the Egyptian king to protect the infant Israelite king, so God can be found in the strangest places, in the least likely people—yes, even among Gentiles.

When the birth narratives of Matthew and Luke are treated as Scripture preserves them, as two different and distinct stories, we discover each gospel's unique perspective on God's revelation in Christ. Instead of creating a mishmash of contradictions by attempting to "harmonize" the gospels as if they were factual, we find that by reading them separately, living in the world of story, each makes perfect sense in itself.

What Kind of Book Is This?

In the wake of the discoveries we are making, it is likely that many who have thought of the Bible as a seamless garment and have taken it literally will now not know which way is up and which down. Such readers are encountering ideas they have simply never heard of before. If at this point these individuals go to the bookstores or library for books that might help make sense of the information being presented, they will discover that these ideas are far from new. They have been known to biblical scholars in some cases for decades and even centuries. Rarely, however, have they been presented in such a manner that the average church member could gain access to them and take advantage of their value for building up instead of tearing down faith.

As our examination of Scripture continues, a new view of the Bible will emerge. But this picture is likely to challenge any preconceived notions of what the Bible is, opening up avenues of thought that call into question the typical understanding of inspiration and the role of Scripture in the development of a meaningful faith. Little by little we shall see that the Bible is indeed an immensely valuable resource for the church, although it may function in a manner quite different from that to which most of us are accustomed.

4.

Blowing the Dust off the Bible

It was over coffee after a church service that a group got into a discussion about the differences in the four gospels. Several members of an Episcopal church had been invited back to one couple's home after the morning service. During the course of conversation the statement was made that whatever differences there might be between the gospels, they are not really important. It was asserted, "The heart of the Christian faith is the empty tomb. All the gospels testify to that. The Christian faith is quite simple, really. It comes down to the bodily resurrection of Jesus."

When it was pointed out that the resurrection accounts in the New Testament are not so straightforward as many assume, and that like other parts of the gospels they contain fundamental differences, the response of one of the guests was immediate: "Keep it simple!" Several of those involved in the discussion heard this as a statement that was intended to close off all discussion of an issue that might threaten the individual's faith.

Many believers yearn for a simple faith, the kind of child-like simplicity that they encountered in their early years of Sunday School. They don't want to complicate it. They point out that the Bible urges upon followers of Jesus a child-like attitude. They remind us that it speaks of the "simplicity" of the gospel. Whenever they hear a sermon that challenges their beliefs, they label it "too deep" for them. They choose never to delve into the Bible in any depth, preferring to "keep it simple."

But the Bible is not a simple book. It is an extremely deep, complex work of literature, the understanding of which can at times be frustratingly difficult. Indeed, the author of the second letter of Peter confirms that the Bible contains teachings that are "hard to understand, which the ignorant and unstable twist to their own destruction, as they do the other scriptures" (2 Pet 3:16), while the author of Hebrews bemoans the fact that at a time when his readers ought to have been ready to teach others, they themselves needed to be instructed all over again in the elementary principles of the gospel.

Far from recommending ignorance, the Scriptures repeatedly urge us to increase our knowledge, our understanding, our wisdom through study. Whatever the "simplicity" of the gospel may be, it is not a justification for lack of knowledge or understanding. In fact when the translators of the King James Version used the word simplicity it conveyed a quite different meaning from what it tends to convey today. It is a word that has nothing to do with the depth of our intellectual questioning of Scripture, and indeed in our time might better be translated "sincerity." One has to wonder how sincere individuals are when they refuse to engage issues that might threaten their childhood or child-like faith.

The longing for a faith that is uncomplicated is understandable in view of the complexity of our modern era. But the wide divergence of opinion even among "simple" folk about what the Bible actually says is ample testimony that there are hurdles to be crossed before what seems like plain English becomes at all plain.

Difficult Words To Hear

Because we wear the spectacles supplied for us by twentieth-century American culture, it is no easy task for us to read the words of even the gospels with the eyes of the first-century listeners to whom they were addressed, let alone those scriptures that emerged centuries earlier. Nineteen hundred years have rolled by since the authors penned these words, so that to focus on them we must blow away a heavy layer of dust that has accumulated over the centuries and obscures their meaning.

We read the Bible in the light of almost two thousand years of church tradition and theological reflection. While this affords us the benefit of the insights of great minds down through the centuries, it also means we have the disadvantage of not being eyewitnesses. Consequently we interpret Scripture according to the particular tradition in which we either grew up or to which we have converted. We judge beliefs to be orthodox or heretical according to the narrow sense of truth and error, right and wrong, that our tradition dictates.

A simple illustration of how the most common and seemingly straightforward of biblical terms are freighted with meaning imparted to them by the tradition in which we have been raised can be seen from the word "sin." Its meaning may seem plain enough to us, but to another equally devoted believer it means something quite different. Seventh Day Adventists might consider themselves to be sinning by working after sunset on Friday evening, while another Christian esteems all days alike. Many Baptists consider it sin to drink a glass of wine, but few Catholics or Episcopalians think of this as sin. The current fundamentalist fervor of the United States appears to focus on sin mostly in terms of sex and the related issues of dress, drink, and dance. Those who are members of the more mainline denominations generally display a much less narrow view of sin. But each group undoubtedly thinks of itself as drawing its viewpoint from Scripture. We are far more deeply affected by our religious heritage, which colors every biblical issue we look at, than we often realize.

Prisoners of Circumstance

A second obstacle we encounter when we read the Bible is that most of us have little awareness of how the circumstances of our lives affect the way we interpret what we read. The significance we ascribe to a particular statement in Scripture is influenced by whether we are male or female, by our race and nationality, our social position, our level of education, our age, our family background, and even the concerns occupying us at a particular moment.

Luke 4:18 furnishes an example of how our place in society comes into play in our reading of the gospels. "The Spirit of the Lord is on me," says Jesus, "because he has anointed me to preach good news to the poor." Those of us living in the affluent West are apt to understand the reference to the poor figuratively: how else can the statement apply to us? We take it to mean the spiritually poor — the humble, by which we mean those who recognize their need of God's help. In that way we become the ones to whom Jesus brought the gospel, since we all need God's help. But in poor countries, millions today interpret the "poor" quite literally. Their impoverished material circumstances furnish them with an entirely different perspective, so that they see Jesus as coming to take their side as the oppressed against the wealthy. Do we who have a roof over our heads and eat well every day have any right to say that their understanding isn't what Luke intended, unless we have known what it is to be unable to feed our families and to watch helplessly as our children die from disease or malnutrition? That Luke did indeed mean the literally poor is made more likely by the way Matthew alters Jesus' description to read "poor in spirit," since he may well have been writing for a relatively successful group of people to whom a statement about being "poor" would have been inapplicable.

Our reading of the gospels is laden with religious and cultural biases. None of us can help it if we are "chips off the old block" not only genetically but also culturally and spiritually. But what we can avoid is the dogmatism that enables us to equate only our preconceived notions with how we understand "the way things really were" back then. We can struggle together to free our minds from the web-like prejudices that keep us enmeshed in the limited worlds that we have each spun for ourselves out of the fabric of our religious traditions and modern life, opening ourselves to investigate thoroughly whatever insight may be available no matter which tradition it comes from. We can acknowledge that each one sees from a unique perspective and can therefore add a dimension of understanding to which we would otherwise remain completely blind. Only in this way do we give ourselves some hope of traveling back in time to hear afresh the words of Scripture.

Two Different Worlds

A third and perhaps far greater barrier to our understanding is that Western civilization is drastically different from the civilization of first century Palestine. The structures of our society have developed along a quite dissimilar path, affecting our family life, homes, and relationships; our jobs, the economy, and the marketplace; our values, traditions, and customs. Life for us bears little resemblance to life in the Middle East in the era when the gospels were composed.

Most of us are vaguely aware that Jesus' world was not the same as ours, but in practice the effect of this is usually limited to a shade of meaning in a word. Essentially we still read the gospels as if they had been written to us. It simply never occurs to us that the evangelists thought in an entirely different way from the way we do in the twentieth century and that what appears to say one thing to us may have meant something entirely different to them.

When we once become alert to the extent to which the Bible is culturally conditioned, we begin to be aware that the images used in Scripture to express the reality of God are images that were meaningful to the people of biblical times and not necessarily to be enshrined eternally in a rigid literalism. For instance, God is depicted as a male because in a patriarchal society the monarch was almost always male. Men held the power in court, army, and temple; and men tended to get away with bossing their families. It would be a mistake to assume that God has male anatomy or thinks and feels only like a male. Just as we interpret the Bible according to our cultural biases, so the biblical authors interpreted their experience of the transcendent through the lenses of Palestinian culture and other Middle Eastern cultures, and in the light of their individual life journeys.

We are prepared now for a fresh understanding of the nature and purpose of Scripture. We are ready to begin learning to read afresh—to hear as best we can the words of the Bible as they were originally intended. This will necessitate paying close attention to detail, as well as not assuming we have heard what is being said, but constantly testing our own hearing against that of others, looking at our conclusions with open minds rather than as if they were cast in concrete.

5.

But Is It *True?*

The nature of a literary work has great bearing upon how one reads it. One reads a scientific work in a different way from *Alice in Wonderland.* An historical novel will bear resemblance to the times that it describes, whereas science fiction may have little or no grounding in reality.

We have seen that the biblical authors were not always factual in their recording of events. But how can we know which of the events they describe really happened? For instance, in proclaiming the message of the Christ, to what extent did the authors deviate from historical fact?

To a lot of us something isn't true if it didn't actually happen. We equate truth and fact, as if for something to be true were identical to its being factual. When reading the Bible it does not seem to occur to us that a story can in itself convey truth.

True to Life

Regardless of how successfully one might feel the book was adapted to the screen, the best selling Australian novel *The Thorn Birds* attracted one of the largest television audiences of all time. People who live in New Zealand, where the novel begins, or in Australia, where the main action takes place, would find it particularly fascinating. Becoming engrossed in this absorbing novel, readers would find themselves living the lives of the characters in their environments. But even if one has never been to New Zealand or Australia, one can experience a genuine taste of life in those surroundings through the characters created by the novelist. The book rings true to life down under in the era in which it was set, as it does also to the struggles of its characters. This then is a book that "speaks to people," particularly those familiar with the setting, in a different way from an Agatha Christie detective story or an imaginative piece of sci-fi. It speaks to us, yet it is not factual.

Jon Dominic Crossan of DePaul University points out that there is a sense in which story characters become more real than actual persons, for they span the ages, and the truths they embody can be understood across centuries and continents. Hamlet and Macbeth still live for us; and psychologists still speak of an Oedipus complex. These fictional characters convey ideas through story that still speak to us today.* The parables of Jesus also introduce us to fictional characters whose experiences embody great truths: they touch our lives without being factual.

Understanding that something can be true without being factual opens up new possibilities for examining biblical literature. Crossan proposes that the story of Jonah is one long parable that poses the question, "What if God does not play the game by our rules?" The message of this piece of fiction is that we expect prophets to obey God and heathen folk such as the Ninevites to disobey, whereas in this story we are surprised by a prophet who disobeys and the heathens who obey. This particular parable is a marvelous way of teaching that God's grace is not bound by our expectations and can work in people's lives in ways we could never imagine, shattering our narrow rules and loosening our rigidity. Crossan concludes that through this parabolic story we are reminded of our finitude and made freshly aware that God does not live in the boxes we construct for him (or her!).

Truth and Fact Are Not the Same

Once we realize that a literary work is not reduced in value simply because it is not wholly factual, we are free to consider

*The Dark Interval, Jon Dominic Crossan (Allen, Texas: Argus Communications, 1975).

whether it might have a different meaning from the meaning generally ascribed to it. We can illustrate this by applying the difference between truth and fact to a modern literary work, George Orwell's *Animal Farm.*

In this classic satire the animals on a farm decide that it is not fair that humans should oppress and use them, so they take over the farm. The idea is to set up a society in which all creatures are equal. But in process of time it turns out that although all animals are equal, some are more equal than others! When decisions need to be made, pigs and horses, it seems, are a lot smarter than certain other animals. So it is that a new hierarchy emerges.

Now let us create a fictional scenario of the future. Imagine that our world is almost totally destroyed in a nuclear holocaust, but that humans survive on some remote part of the planet. Little literature comes through this nightmare, but one work which does is *Animal Farm.* As the world goes through a dark age of primitive conditions akin to those of the Dark Ages many centuries ago, when superstitious Europeans incorporated stone resting places for witches into the outer walls of their houses lest the witches seek repose within, people begin to look upon *Animal Farm* as the story of a wondrous age in the dim and distant past when animals actually talked!

But two thousand years into the future, following a second Enlightenment, archaeologists begin to unearth from the rubble of the twentieth century a great mass of literature that was contemporary with *Animal Farm.* In this literature, historians learn for the first time about a system that ruled over the lives of a large portion of the world's population in our century. No one knew there had ever been such a phenomenon as totalitarianism prior to this discovery. Suddenly a literary scholar analyzing the writings of the totalitarian rulers that have been unearthed from ruins that were once Moscow sees in that system a whole new meaning for *Animal Farm.* He announces to the world of the fortieth century that this beloved book is not in fact history but a satire that gives insight into the inherent problems of totalitarianism. In effect it is an expose of totalitarianism in the 1930s and '40s. While many want to hang on to a literal interpretation of this work that they have so long treasured as a literal record of a past era, the world of scholarship in the fortieth century now sees it as true but not factual. And while contemplating a wondrous age in which even animals could talk may be tantalizing to some, to understand *Animal Farm*'s hidden meaning has for scholars become of far greater value for avoiding the perils of political systems, because it speaks to life as we experience it.

Many biblical stories are like *Animal Farm*. They are true, though not historically accurate or factual. They are concerned with proclaiming a message, not with providing us with a chronology of events from the history of Israel or the life of Jesus of Nazareth. We must learn to read them not as history but as message.

6.

A Lesson from a Famous Pig

God does not live exclusively in the time-space framework in which we enact the drama of our lives. If God did live in our world, God would be just another thing, not the one in whom, as the apostle Paul expressed it, "we live and move and have our being." God could not be the ground of our being were God merely another being alongside us. The world is infused with God, but God transcends the world. How then are we to experience this transcendent God?

Jon Dominic Crossan offers us a wonderful illustration from sailing of how we encounter the infinite. For him the thrill of sailing lies in beating as close to the eye of the wind as possible, so that the boat heels over and strains hard. But it is not possible to sail into the eye of the wind, for in the eye of the wind the sails go limp. We can only sail as close as possible into the wind. So too our finitude keeps us from directly facing the infinite and therefore invisible God who encompasses the billions of galaxies that form the universe. All our statements about God are but figures of speech, not accurate descriptions of God. We cannot capture in finite words the one who is infinite. And yet it is through words that God becomes present to us. We encounter the transcendent through words that push meaningful language to its extremes. It is at the edges of language, in the world of story, that God becomes present to us.

It is in metaphors that we reach the edges of language and may encounter the transcendent. The invisible, incorporeal, immense God of the creeds reaches us through metaphorical words, through story.

Two Kinds of Language

If we are to decode the biblical narratives, we must begin to read in a new way the actual language used by the writers.

In E.B. White's delightful children's story *Charlotte's Web,* Wilbur the famous pig discovers that a barn can be a lonely place and goes in search of a friend to play with. The goose is expecting goslings, so she can't leave her eggs. When he asks the lamb to play with him, the lamb answers, "Certainly not. In the first place, I cannot get into your pen, as I am not old enough to jump over the fence. In the second place, I am not interested in pigs. Pigs mean less than nothing to me."

"What do you mean, less than nothing?" replies Wilbur. "I don't think there is any such thing as less than nothing. Nothing is absolutely the limit of nothingness. It's the lowest you can go. It's the end of the line. How can something be less than nothing? If there were something less than nothing, then nothing would not be nothing, it would be something: even though it's just a very little bit of something. But if nothing is nothing, then nothing has nothing that is less than it is."

Wilbur would have had great difficulty reading both *Animal Farm* and the Bible. Wilbur, you see, could only understand language in one way. He took everything literally.

But in fact language can be divided into two types: steno language and tensive language. A stenographer takes down exactly what is said, without interpretation. Steno language, which is used predominantly, for example, by scientists, relates to facts, objects, and definitions. It is the kind of language in which every word is carefully defined and usually means only one thing. Tensive language, on the other hand, employs words in such a way as to generate tension. This is the language characteristic of the artistic community, the language of poetry, metaphor, and symbol. It is a language that was foreign to Wilbur.

Truth That's Found in Meaning

Tensive language can convey truth in ways that steno language is incapable of because of the latter's precise and therefore limited meaning. We could illustrate this power of tensive language in a more dramatic way with any number of poems. Perhaps you know such a work. We think, for example, of Edith Sitwell's *Still Falls the Rain.*

A student of modern English literature may recognize in the poem a description of bombs falling on London in 1940. By means of the tensive language employed in the poem, this horrifying event is cast in a new light: it takes on significance that no straight historical account of the same event could give it. In a single wordplay such as that on the word "rain," images are invoked of the rain of bombs, the splashing of tears of grief at such human suffering, the dripping of the Christ's blood as he died to end injustice, the blood that is spilled in warfare, and the reign (spelled differently but heard the same) of terror that held sway over Europe in this dark hour. Human beings, like animals, are suffering in this reign of terror: like the wounded, baited bear; the blind, weeping bear whom the keepers beat; or the tears (and perhaps here also we have a wordplay) of the hunted hare as it is torn to pieces by the hounds, its cries unheeded. Even the word "still" may carry the triple meaning of rain falling silently, unceasingly, and seemingly endlessly. The poem is rich in meaning and we could analyze it at many levels, like peeling the layers of an onion, to unveil the meaning compacted into each phrase, gaining new insights as we penetrate deeper. Though fully rooted in history, it relates that history in such a manner as to transcend the limitations of literal, steno language.

To treat tensive language as steno language renders it sterile and is idolatrous. This was of course the problem with Wilbur, for he could hear only steno language. By being so literal in our use of words, we fail to understand what is being communicated. We miss the breath of inspiration, the insight an individual has been given by the Creator, because we idolize the words themselves. To read Scripture in such a way is akin to poring over a musical score like Handel's *Messiah* seeking to locate its inspiration, without ever hearing, with our mind's ear or real ear, the oratorio performed and allowing ourselves to be grasped by the music and transported into ecstasy.

As with poetry, much of biblical literature contains layers of meaning compressed into terse, tensive narratives. (In fact, though it is often lost in translation, much of the Bible *is* poetry.) The text itself is like an iceberg. What protrudes above the surface is the words of the text, while the main world of the text lies hidden from view as the bulk of an iceberg remains hidden under water. We must look beneath the surface words to the deeper meanings that these words seek to convey. Just as we have to ponder over the meaning of the poet's metaphors, what needs to be done with the biblical stories and poetry is to unpack the significance of the authors' cryptic statements, bringing to light a richness of teaching that will remain frozen in literalism as long as we, like Wilbur, fail to appreciate how the biblical authors used language.

7.

How To Read a Gospel

Through biblical stories and poetry we encounter the transcendent God. It is in this meeting with that which is ultimate that the kingdom of God becomes reality for us.

Jesus proclaimed the reign of God in human lives. To come under the reign of God is to have our humanly built world shattered and to enter into the new age, the new creation, the new humanity that God is bringing into being.

Matthew, Mark, Luke, and John use story to paint a picture of the ending of one world and the dawning of a new world. In the story world of the gospels, at the cross the old world order collapsed into primordial chaos. At the resurrection a new world, a new creation, peopled by a new kind of human, began rising out of the embers of the old world's destruction. The gospels are a proclamation of the fact that this has happened, and an invitation to each of us to allow our personal worlds to be transformed by God's new world.

Readers to whom the ideas presented in this book are new may be experiencing something similar to this at this very moment. They are in shock. They feel their foundations shaking, their world beginning to crumble, and they are wondering what will replace their old world view. The authors of this present work are not unfamiliar with this feeling. It took a long time for each of us to digest a new view of the Bible.

The reign of God comes to each of us as God shatters our world then builds a new world for us from the pictures in the gospels painted by metaphor. The process of tearing down our old world and building a new world is both painful and slow. The rebuilding is piece by piece, much like newborn infants build their world one piece at a time. The gospels, using the limits of language, employ story to enable us to see what the new creation is like. They give us a picture of the new world God's reign in our lives ushers in. Not only do they give us a new vision, a new sense of perspective, but they also present us with the keys to enter that new world. Through their stories we are transformed and the new creation becomes a reality for us.

What matters for us is not debates over the precise historical events that may lie back of these literary works, but that we enter into the encounter with the transcendent that is captured in their stories. For it is in so doing that language puts on flesh, the transcendent impinges, and God is present among human beings today as in Jesus over 1900 years ago.

Unpacking the Meaning of a Gospel Story

To illustrate this we turn to the Gospel of John, the Fourth Gospel. While the other gospels contain a great many stories of Jesus' mighty deeds, this gospel is built around seven signs. These are the only miracle stories in this gospel. We might use any one of them to illustrate how tensive language conveys meaning at levels not immediately obvious, but the story of the wedding at Cana is particularly apt because it sets the tone for the rest of the gospel, introducing a theme that will be played out again and again through the different signs the author incorporates into his narrative.

The medieval alchemists would have gone wild had they been in Cana. To alter one substance into another was their dream. Had we the power to do that we could end the plight of the poor and hungry right now. But is the story of the wedding at Cana really intended to portray Jesus as the ultimate alchemist with magical powers over the elements? If so, it is difficult to make sense of Jesus' final discourse on the eve of his crucifixion, when he says, "Truly, truly, I say to you, those who believe in me will also do the works that I do; and greater works than

these will they do, because I go to the Father." We are to do
even greater works than Jesus himself did because he is now
enthroned with the Creator and empowering the community of
believers through the Spirit. But if we are talking about literally
turning water into wine, we don't see too many of us doing even
that, let alone greater things. So what does this story mean for
those of us who have to deal with the real problems of life that
face the world of the twenty-first century, problems that don't
seem to be solved by pronouncing magical formulae or waving
a wand?

The text labels the changing of the water into wine a sign. A
sign points away from itself to something else, to a reality that
is not immediately visible. Suppose a family from New York who
has never been to Chicago decides to visit Chicago. Nearing
Chicago they see a sign, "Chicago, eighty miles." "Chicago!"
they exclaim and pitch camp for the night. Next morning they
head back to New York reporting that no one lives in Chicago
any longer.

A sign points us to a reality, but it does not itself constitute
the reality. To pitch camp at the Chicago sign as if that were
Chicago is to miss the reality. But that is exactly what happens
when the modern reader hears the story of the marriage at Cana.
To literalize the sign as if all it were about is how Jesus rescued
a newly married couple from the embarrassment of running out
of wine, instead of searching for what the sign points to, is to
miss the point.

At the outset the author gives us an important clue to the
meaning of the story: "On the third day there was a marriage
at Cana in Galilee" (Jn 2:1). When we are not even told what
dates Jesus lived or the years in which his ministry took place,
what does it matter which day this wedding was on? Why include
such a finicky detail? Besides, which third day does he mean?
The third day of the week? the month? the year?

To catch the significance of the third day we have to go back
to chapter one. If we take day one as the day of Jesus' baptism,
then reference is made to day two, the day following the baptism,
in verse 29. Yet another day is spoken of in verse 35, which
would be day three, the day on which Jesus calls his first two
disciples. Then there's a fourth day in verse 43, on which Jesus

calls Philip and Nathanael to follow him and decides to set out for Galilee. Clearly the reference to the third day isn't the third day after Jesus' baptism because by now we are well past day three. It might mean the third day after Jesus arrived in Cana, but the text nowhere says so.

Yet the author insists that what took place in Cana was on the third day. And not just any third day, but emphatically, as the Greek puts it, *the* third day. In chapter one the author does not number the days but simply speaks of them as "the next day." But now, unexpectedly, he throws in a number and it doesn't fit the sequence of days given up to this point. After repeatedly using the expression "the next day," this reference to the third day draws our attention. Could it be that the author is deliberately trying to draw attention to the number three?

This is not the only third day on which Jesus does something significant in Cana. In chapter four we read, "After two days he departed to Galilee." *After two days* is a Hebraism meaning on the third day. We find the expression in Hosea, where God says to Israel through the prophet, "After two days I will heal you, on the third day I will raise you up" (Hos 6:2). So in one scriptural passage the third day has to do with being raised up. As the apostle Paul writes to the Corinthians, "For I delivered to you as of first importance what I also received, that Christ died for our sins in accordance with the scriptures, that he was buried, that he was raised on the third day in accordance with the scriptures" (I Cor 15:3-4). There is no scripture in the Old Testament that says in so many words that the Messiah would be killed and raised on the third day. But three is the number of redemption, deliverance, liberation, restoration, resurrection. It is a symbol of new beginnings.

On his second visit to Cana, this second third day, Jesus is met by an official whose son is dying (4:43-54). What is the second sign that Jesus performs? Raising up the official's son from his deathbed. Just as we might expect, since it occurs on the third day, it is a resurrection story. Could it be that the evangelist begins his story of the first sign at Cana with a reference to the third day because he wants to alert us in code that this, too, is a resurrection story? Is it possible that the story of the marriage is a sign that points toward resurrection?

Jesus' mother points out that the guests at the wedding have run out of wine. How does he answer her? "And Jesus said to her, 'O Woman, what have you to do with me? My hour has not yet come.'" Many have pondered why Jesus uttered such a strange statement. What is the connection between running out of wine and his "hour," whatever that may be, not yet having come?

The author of John refers to this hour several times in the gospel. But until we get to chapter twelve, which is on the eve of Jesus' death, this mysterious "hour" that is referred to is always placed in the future. Only when his death is impending, and specifically when Greeks "wish to see Jesus" (12:20-23), anticipating the Gospel's threatening redefinition of Israel opposed by the Gospel's Judeans ("Jews"), do we hear Jesus say, "The hour has come." He is referring to the hour of his death. So Jesus ties the running out of the wine to his death.

There is an aspect of Jesus' crucifixion that is unique to the Fourth Gospel. In Matthew, when Jesus is crucified they offer him wine to drink, mingled with gall. But the text says, "When he had tasted it, he would not drink it." Later someone tries to offer it again, but others tell him to wait, and Jesus dies without drinking it. So too Mark records, "And they offered him wine mingled with myrrh; but he did not take it." Likewise in Luke. In these three gospels the mixture Jesus is offered has a pain-deadening effect. The evangelists make the point that Jesus doesn't drink it because they want to portray him in command until the last moment, his senses in no way dulled. He is coenthroned with the Creator, reigning from the cross as "King of kings."

But in the Fourth Gospel it isn't painkiller that Jesus is offered. The author writes, "After this Jesus, knowing that all was now finished . . . said, 'I thirst.' A bowl full of vinegar stood there; so they put a sponge full of the vinegar on hyssop and held it to his mouth. When Jesus had received the vinegar, he said, 'It is finished'; and he bowed his head and gave up his spirit." The Greek word for "vinegar" means sour wine. The wine that is talked about here is wine from the end of the barrel, the dregs.

The sour wine is offered on hyssop. The mention of hyssop

is significant. In Matthew, Mark, and Luke the Last Supper takes place the evening of Passover, so that Jesus is crucified during the daylight hours of the first day of the feast of the Passover. But in John there is no Last Supper—no Passover meal in an upper room, no institution of the symbols of bread and wine. The entire discourse of John 13-17 takes place in the context of an ordinary meal *before* the feast of the Passover, and Jesus is executed the day before Passover. In John, Jesus is already dead and buried before Matthew, Mark, and Luke's Last Supper. John emphasizes that his body was removed from the gallows and placed in a tomb before Passover began at sunset. In Exodus, concerning the Passover we read: "Take a bunch of hyssop and dip it in the blood which is in the basin, and touch the lintel and the two doorposts with the blood . . ." (Ex 12:22). The Passover was a moment of liberation, when God raised Israel up out of a living death and set them apart to be God's own people. Like the third day, hyssop sounds a death and resurrection theme, and the creation of a new Israel which includes "Greeks."

At the wedding in Cana, what triggers Jesus' comment about his impending hour of execution? It is his mother's statement that the wine has run out. All that is left in the barrel is the dregs, the sour wine. It is this that Jesus will drink moments before his death. In his death he will symbolically consume the dregs of the old wine that ran out at the marriage in Cana.

The old wine represents the old Israel, which in the writer's view had run its course. It is a symbol of the Judean rulers ("Jews") as the writer understood them. When that Israel has spent itself and done its worst—when the old wine runs out—it ends up crucifying the very one who models what true humanness is. The new, definitive human being is on the cross paying for being so radically different from the old humanity in which all of us have participated. And this paschal act liberates us from the old so that we might enter into the new with him.

In contrast, the new wine celebrates the new humanity that is present in Jesus. And from what does Jesus create the celebration wine? Out of six stone jars that were used for the Judean rites of purification. Jesus takes the identity that has bound us and makes us merry with new wine. Like the first Christians who

received the Spirit of Jesus on the day of Pentecost, when we
imbibe this new wine we become so freed up that those tied to
religious rules do not understand our celebrating and imagine
we are drunk.

Truth To Live By

The church is described in the book of the Revelation, the
last book in the New Testament, as the bride of the Lamb. The
wedding at Cana is a picture of what the Revelation calls the
marriage feast of the Lamb, the celebration of a marriage in
which humanity and divinity are united together as one. The
imagery is drawn from Isaiah, who says of this marriage feast,

> The Lord of hosts will make for all peoples a feast of fat
> things, a feast of wine on the lees [well-aged wine], of fat
> things full of marrow, of wine on the lees well refined. And
> he will destroy . . . the covering that is cast over all peoples,
> the veil that is spread over all nations. He will swallow up
> death for ever [note the resurrection theme], and the Lord
> God will wipe away tears from all faces . . . (Isa 25:6-8)

As Jesus dies, the old wine gives out, having done its worst.
Humanity's nit-picking, small-minded, narrow religious views
are rendered powerless by his death on the cross. Religiosity no
longer has power to bind us. Its strictures and taboos are swal-
lowed up by the feasting and rejoicing of the marriage of the
Lamb. With Jesus in our midst we are liberated to become truly
human, no longer living in fear that God, whom so many view
as akin to a tyrant, is out to get us if we put a foot wrong.

It is to this new relationship between humans and God that
Hosea refers. Through the prophet God says: "In that day . . .
you will call me, 'My husband,' and no longer will you call me,
'My Baal' " (2:16). Baal means lord. Humanity is entering into
a relationship with God that is one of love instead of lordship.
We are placed on an equal footing with God, no longer subservient. "I will betroth you to me in righteousness and in justice,
in steadfast love, and in mercy. I will betroth you to me in faith-

fulness; and you shall know the Lord." We may not know our boss, but we do know the one to whom we are married. God wants a close relationship with us, just like that of newlyweds. Hosea's words are picked up by Jesus in his discourse on the eve of his crucifixion: "No longer do I call you servants," he explains, "for the servant does not know what his master is doing; but I have called you friends . . . " (Jn 15:15). Once again we note the emphasis on knowing God's intentions, as in Hosea. No matter that we may want to keep God at a distance, God is determined not to remain in a superior position but to be our equal on a level footing. Friends, not servants; husband, not lord.

"In that day," God says through Hosea, "I will answer the heavens and they shall answer the earth; and the earth shall answer the grain, the wine, and the oil." Through those who have entered into this marriage with the Creator, the whole earth is to experience renewal. God will work through us to bring about an era of universal prosperity, an age of feasting, a time of celebration. Hunger and poverty, drought and famine, flood and pestilence, death and destruction are to be conquered, giving way to a world in which all humans live well.

The sign at Cana points us to the union of God with humanity that is actualized in Jesus. When Jesus answers his mother that his hour has not yet come, in fact it hasn't. But he acts as though it already has. He acts as if what his death brings about is already true. He celebrates the new relationship at the beginning of his ministry and subsequently will act as though the marriage of the Lamb is already a reality. The way he will live throughout the Fourth Gospel is predicated on God and humanity already being joined as one.

He lives out of that ever-present reality, although it is invisible. This is how, later in the gospel, he can tell Martha after her brother Lazarus has died, "I am the resurrection and the life." And we will hear him say that all who believe in him and participate with him in the new humanity, which is a divine humanity, fashioned in the image of the Creator, have already passed from death to life. In other words, we are already enjoying eternal life, already living a life that has been raised up into the divine and fused with the life of the Creator. That is the meaning of our baptism. We have died to the old religion with its taboos and guilt trips and been raised up into the freedom of the life of God.

It may not be apparent to us in everyday life that we have been raised up into the life of God. When life weighs heavily upon us we are frequently unaware that we have been divinized like Jesus. But we are called to believe it is true even though we cannot see it, and to act as if it were so. Once awareness that we have been united with God becomes the overarching reality in our lives we can take anything that life may deal out to us, even crucifixion. We can handle the dregs because we have the power to "turn water into wine," to create new possibilities in freedom where there seems to be no hope, to bring about a reason for celebrating even when everyone else is in despair. No matter what life may throw at us, we recognize that its force has been spent. Its power to hurt us is temporary and limited. The old wine has run out. Already the new is beginning to flow and God is in process of wiping away all tears from our eyes. The celebration of the marriage of the Lamb has begun.

Our new relationship with God is brought out in the Fourth Gospel's account of Easter through a story that is not found in any other gospel. The resurrected Jesus appears to Mary, who imagines he is the gardener. As he speaks her name, she recognizes him. The text says, "She turned and said to him in Hebrew, 'Rabboni' " — and a scribe has added, "which means Teacher." But it is Rabbi that means teacher, not Rabboni. Rabboni is a different word, the very word used in an Aramaic targum (translation) of Hosea to mean husband. The text of the targum says, "On that day you will call me Rabboni ... " On the day to which Hosea points, Mary, representative of all believers, recognizes her new relationship with God by throwing her arms around the exalted Jesus, now divinized, and calling him Rabboni, Husband, borrowing the language of Hosea.

Jesus tells Mary, "Do not hold me." The Greek means, "Do not keep holding on to me," signifying not mere touch but clinging. Mary's relationship with Jesus has been subservient but she is no longer to cling as a dependent. She is to be friend, not servant; he is to be husband, not overlord. As God raised Jesus up into divinity, so the Christ through the community that is his body raises people up out of the living death in which they are entombed.

Read as metaphor, the first sign of the Fourth Gospel prompts us to ask whether the church is indeed the community of the resurrection. Is it like a joyous party? Does it celebrate the uniting of God and humanity? Does it foster subservience and dependence with respect to God, or equality and partnership? Through tensive language, the author has conveyed a message that spans the centuries and challenges the church in every age. It is a message much more meaningful than a mere recounting of a biographical detail from the life of Jesus.

Part **2**

HOW WE GOT
THE BIBLE

8.

Is the Bible

a Seamless Garment?

The intent of the gospels is not to chronicle the events of Jesus' life but to address issues of importance to the community of which the writer was a member. The authors had a message to convey, for which task they employed standard literary techniques of the time. It was the message, not historical accuracy or scientific fact, that was of importance to them. When this is understood, it is evident why there are differences between the gospels.

Once one begins to notice the differences between the gospels, it is a short step to observing that differences exist throughout the Old Testament also. But here the differences are not only between books, they are frequently within the same book. Sometimes contradictory statements appear within a few chapters of each other, at times even within a few verses.

How did the differences within a book arise? The answer to this mystery will open the way for us to reconstruct how we got the Bible.

The differences within a single Old Testament book can readily be seen from one of the first biblical stories many of us learned as children in Sunday school, the tale of David and Goliath.

The way it is told to us, King Saul was at war with the Philistines, and David the shepherd boy came to the battlefield to bring provisions to his brothers who were serving in Saul's army. David began mouthing off about his ability to slay the giant, and eventually his bragging came to the ears of the king. Thus it was that David met Saul and, after lopping off the giant's head, became the king's armor bearer and personal musician. Whenever the king was troubled, David would play the lyre to calm him.

Few notice in reading the story of David and Saul that the text says both that David was a confidant of Saul long before the incident with Goliath of Gath, and that it was through the battle with Goliath that David met Saul for the first time. These are two conflicting accounts of how David met Saul.

If one follows the sequence of I Samuel, in chapter 16 Saul was tormented by an evil spirit and summoned his servants to seek out a skilled musician to soothe his troubled mind. One of them told the king, "I have seen a son of Jesse the Bethlehemite, who is skillful in playing, a man of valor, a man of war, prudent in speech, and a man of good presence; and the Lord is with him." Upon hearing this, Saul sent messengers to David's father Jesse to ask that David be released from tending the flocks so that he might enter Saul's service. "And David came to Saul," we are told, "and entered his service." Saul was well pleased with David's work and wanted to retain David on a permanent basis, so "Saul sent to Jesse, saying, 'Let David remain in my service, for he has found favor in my sight.'" David no longer tended sheep for his father: he was Saul's full-time personal assistant. The text makes the specific point that Saul and David enjoyed a close relationship: "And Saul loved him greatly, and he became his armor-bearer."

The next event in the sequence of I Samuel, told in chapter 17, is the war against the Philistines. In this scene David is still at home tending sheep for his father. There is no mention of his employment with Saul. He does not meet Saul until the battle with Goliath.

In attempting to reconcile the story of David meeting Saul through Goliath with the fact that he was already Saul's musician and armor-bearer, it might be suggested that David must have left Saul's employ because a war was raging: he had simply returned to working for his father for the duration of the war. If he was Saul's armor-bearer, this makes little sense; nevertheless, let us explore this argument further.

In chapter 17 David goes back and forth from Saul's armies taking food from Bethlehem to the three enlisted brothers. It is on one such visit that he learns about Goliath and inquires as to what sort of reward will be given to the one who conquers the giant. He is told that anyone who kills Goliath will be rewarded with riches, marriage to the king's daughter, and the free status of his father's house. David is quick to boast of his ability to slay the giant.

Hearing of his braggadocio, David's oldest brother becomes angry. "Why have you come down?" demands the brother. "And with whom have you left those few sheep in the wilderness? I know your presumption, and the evil of your heart; for you have come down to see the battle." Most of us have read this passage many times. But did we ever stop to ponder the strangeness of Eliab's attitude toward David in view of the fact that in the previous chapter David is Saul's personal armor-bearer? Would this eldest brother not *expect* David to be at the battle? If David is already in Saul's immediate battle entourage, why does his brother denigrate him as fit only for minding a few sheep?

If we read on, the mystery intensifies. When David's claims of gallantry reach the ears of Saul, he is summoned before the king. David assures Saul that he can slay the giant and recounts his experience of grappling with wild animals. Saul thinks the lad is crazy and tells him to go get himself killed if he is intent on so doing. Note carefully that there is no indication that Saul already knows David. Indeed, Saul shows him his armor, which is clearly strange to David—a surprising fact if he is Saul's armor-bearer.

That Saul has never set eyes on David before becomes patent in the wake of David's routing of the Philistines. When David triumphs over the giant, Saul asks the commander of the army, "Abner, whose son is this youth?" To which the commander replies, "As your soul lives, O king, I cannot tell." Saul then instructs Abner, "Inquire whose son the stripling is." Only now do Saul and his commander learn that David is the son of Jesse the Bethlehemite. Until this moment David is completely unknown to Saul.

How are we to account for the fact that in I Samuel 16 David is brought into Saul's employ, functions as his personal musician and armor-bearer, yet is a total stranger to both Saul and the commander of the army a chapter later?

Most of us who have grown up in Sunday School have read the various books of the Bible as if they were all of a piece. In fact we have seen the Bible itself as a seamless garment, the authors writing in direct response to the inspiration of God. But now we are faced with the fact that there are in I Samuel 16 and 17, interwoven into a single story, two entirely separate and conflicting accounts of how David met Saul. Not only is the Bible as a whole not all of a piece, but individual books also contain accounts that are irreconcilably in conflict.

When this puzzle was presented to a Sunday School class of seven- and eight-year-old children, after some discussion they concluded that two different stories, composed by different authors, had been joined together. It does not require much detective work to discover that two traditions have been sewn into a single garment by a later editor — a garment whose seams are still evident to the careful reader.

In the wake of this discovery, we might begin rereading the Bible from the beginning. What else have we missed? Perhaps the Bible is a very different kind of book from what we have imagined.

9.

Assembling the Pieces
of the Jigsaw Puzzle

The process of writing, rewriting, and editing the documents that now appear in the Bible took place over many hundreds of years — in fact, over a *thousand* years. During the course of these centuries, the different books appeared at various stages of composition. Some of these compositions became frozen in time and were handed down to us as distinct books much as they appear in our Bible today. Others continued to be reworked, eventually becoming part of larger documents. The earlier stages of composition of these larger works are no longer readily apparent. However, they can be discovered by careful analysis of the books as they appear today. Through such analysis, we can see how they have grown over the ages.

How the Bible evolved can be seen from its opening stories. It is common to read the story of Adam and Eve in the garden of Eden as an elaboration of the creation of male and female on the sixth day of the Genesis 1 creation story. To one who has grown up believing in the literal truth of Scripture there is no other way to view these two chapters.

Once we are aware that the Bible contains differing accounts of the same events, we are able to see what it had been forbidden to see before: that the story of creation in seven days and the story of the garden of Eden are mutually exclusive. To accept one as fact is to reject automatically the historicity of the other. Many who read the Bible regularly have missed the fact that right at the beginning of the Bible, in Genesis 1 and 2, there are *two entirely separate accounts of creation.*

Two Different Stories

Genesis 1 begins with a world shrouded in water. In the view of the ancients, not only in Palestine but elsewhere in the Mediterranean and Near Eastern world, the universe was full of water. This is why the sky is blue. There was no concept of space with galaxies light years apart. In creating the world, God created a sort of bubble in the water, placing over this bubble a translucent dome (the "firmament"), so that the waters below were separated from the watery universe above. All of the heavenly bodies were not far above our heads, revolving on the dome that kept the watery "blue beyond" out.

The next thing God did was to gather the waters below into seas so that dry land appeared. In this dry ground God planted vegetation. Following this, fish and birds were created on the fifth day. Then on the sixth day God created animals, followed by the simultaneous creation of male and female at the close of that day. The story ends with a sabbath of rest. This creation account ends in Genesis 2:3. Chapters and verses, of course, were not a part of the original text, having been added in recent centuries to make it easier to locate biblical texts.

After a new heading, Genesis 2:4 continues: "In the day that the Lord God made the earth and the heavens, when no plant of the field was yet in the earth and no herb of the field had yet sprung up . . . then the Lord God formed a human of dirt from the ground . . ." This is the opening statement of a second creation story.

In this second creation story the scene is not a watery universe but a dry earth that experiences no rain and is watered by what the King James Version of the Bible calls a "mist" (more likely some sort of "flow") that comes up from the ground. So this story begins not with water but with dry ground. This is quite in contrast to the creation of the world out of a watery universe in chapter 1.

The next event in this second creation story is the creation of a human. Unlike the first creation story, all of this is before there is any vegetation. Only subsequent to the making of the human does God cause the ground to produce vegetation and the human receives a home in a particular garden.

The second creation story states that the female of the human species was created because God thought the first human needed an equivalent partner. God first tried to satisfy this need by creating one animal after another, until the entire animal kingdom had been created. Only when this failed to meet the human's need for a partner did God create woman.

If the second creation account is simply an expansion of the creation story in chapter 1, it is not likely that God thought the human needed a partner, because the human was not created until well into the sixth day. The human would have had but a few hours to admire the wonders of creation — rivers, trees, flowers, plants of every description upon which his eyes had never before been cast, and plenty of animals to keep him company. In the Genesis 1 story, as we have seen, the animal kingdom was in existence before the human was created.

It makes a lot more sense that the second creation story is an entirely different account. In Sunday school material depicting this event, the animals are invariably portrayed as being created simultaneously, then paraded past Adam. It is emphasized that only Genesis "kinds" were created — that is, the basic species, not all of the many varieties within a species. These varieties, literalists allow, sprang up later and continue to do so today. Still, even if we are talking about basic species, a huge array of creatures is involved. The narrative implies that as God assessed Adam's situation, God decided that the solution was to create a "help corresponding to" Adam. The expression "corresponding to" means as like as possible. So God proceeded to attempt to create a creature that would be sufficiently similar to Adam to be helpful to him. As Adam had been made out of dirt, so this helpful creature was also fashioned from dirt. Each of God's various attempts to create a creature that would fit the bill was brought to Adam, and God listened to see how Adam would name them. Let us assume that the crocodile was the first creature to be made. As God listened, "crocodile" and "human" did not correspond at all. So perhaps God then tried a cow. Again, as God listened, "cow" and "human" bore no resemblance. In the view of this second creation story, all of the world's species came into existence as God attempted to make from the dirt a creature that would correspond to the human, without actually being human. Finally, at the conclusion of this seemingly endless sequence of creating a new kind of animal each time Adam tired of the latest attempt and longed for something more alike to which to relate, God tumbled to the idea of making "woman," which sounds like "human" (there is a word play in Hebrew as well) not from dirt, but from a rib taken from Adam himself. The lengthy process of creating animals and humans in this chapter stands in radical contrast to the instantaneous and simultaneous creation in the Genesis 1 story.

Indeed the differences between the two accounts are startling. The sequence of the second story almost reverses the sequence of the first. In Genesis 1 the vegetation comes first; in Genesis 2 Adam is created before any vegetation. In Genesis 1 the animals precede the creation of Adam; in Genesis 2 the animals are created after Adam in a long sequence. In Genesis 1 man and woman are created together on the sixth day; in Genesis 2 a human is created, then all the animals, and only after this lengthy process does woman appear on the scene. As with the story of David and Goliath, it becomes apparent that two quite separate stories have been joined together to form the introduction to the book of Genesis.

What Creation Stories Are About

Once we recognize that there are different creation stories, we realize that the Genesis authors never intended what they wrote to be understood as a factual history of how the universe and our world came into being. They were not writing about the origin of our world in the sense of how matter came into existence and took its present shape. In discussing how the world came into being, they had a very different kind of "world" in mind.

The word "world" has more than one meaning. There is *the* world, the physical planet on which we live. There is the Western world and there is the Third World, both of which are worlds apart. But there is also the business world, the jazz world, the sports world, your world, and our world, our individual worlds.

We are familiar with the use of "world," as distinct from "globe," in the expression "it was the end of an era, the end of a world." We say that we "live in a different world" from that of the last century. We regret that a friend's "world came to an end" when his wife died. And we are accustomed to saying, "It's a whole new world." It is this use of the word "world" that is predominant in the Bible.

The "world" as each of us engages it is not precisely the same "world" our fellow voyagers on spaceship earth encounter. A person's world emerges from the relationship between the individual and society. Our identity is rooted in the culture in which we live. Through the way in which we relate as unique individuals to our society and our culture, each of us builds for ourselves a world of our own.

Reality for a homeless single mother is different from reality for a corporate executive whose days involve countless meetings, business lunches, cocktail parties, and a social whirlwind. Their lives are worlds apart. A New Yorker's world is not the same as the world of a person who is Oregon-born and bred. Neither is the world of an American identical to the world of a French person, a Russian, a West African.

Analysis of what we know as the "world" is the domain of specialists such as geographers, oceanographers, volcanologists, seismologists, botanists, biologists, geologists, and a host of other experts. For those who grew up thinking of the Bible as akin to a scientific textbook—indeed as the basis of all true science—it is a surprise to learn that it actually has little to say about the objective world and does not deal with how this world came into being or how it works. The author of the first chapter of Genesis skips over the creation of the material universe. The priestly writer who composed the creation story did not have the tools of modern science to unravel the mysteries of this creative event, nor was how our planet came into being his primary concern. The focus shifts in a few brief statements to the world of human beings, which is what occupies the rest of his work. His interest was in how our subjective worlds are built—how each of us builds our own world.

Our world has much to do with our ideas—with how we see life. In World War II, Americans, British, French, Germans, Russians, and Japanese each saw reality in a different manner. The history each tells of that war is drastically different. It's as if each nation inhabited a different world. The differences are highlighted by contrasting the Japanese kamikaze pilot who had sworn allegiance to his emperor as to a god with an American GI who thought nothing of hooking trout from the Emperor's private pool in the Imperial Palace as the war came to a close. What shocks one is a game to another.

In a similar way the two most famous of biblical creation stories are about how people in a particular Middle Eastern society viewed life at two different periods in the history of that society. The stories are about *their* worlds.

A Question of Authorship

Most of us have grown up believing that Moses wrote all five books of what is known as the Torah, the beginning of the Bible, with its stories of creation, the Flood, the patriarchs Abram, Isaac and Jacob, and the Exodus. Once we realize that the creation stories of Genesis 1 and 2 come from different hands and are about the meaning of life for ancient peoples rather than about the actual origin of the earth, the question of how the earliest parts of the Bible came to be written looms large. If Moses did not write the books that form the bedrock of the first part of the Bible, who did? And why are they presented *as if* Moses wrote them?

Until about two hundred years ago it was assumed that the earliest part of the Bible to be written was the creation story in Genesis 1. But careful analysis of the two different creation accounts led historians to conclude that the story of Adam and Eve in the Garden of Eden was written up to four centuries before the seven-day creation story of Genesis 1.

How and why the earliest stories of the Bible came to be written, and how the Bible was gradually put together, is the topic to which we now turn. The process by which the first five books of the Bible were composed illustrates how much of ancient literature came into being. It is typical of the way most of the rest of the Bible was written. In the following chapters we sketch an outline of this process. Understanding this process will be critical for making sense of the Bible's earliest stories.

10.

How Did the Bible Come

To Be Written?

Who began the Bible? To answer this question it will be helpful for us to have some knowledge of the significance of writing in the ancient world.

In an era when printing presses and photocopiers reproduce written material for every conceivable purpose, it is hard for us to imagine a time when writing was not commonplace and served only a very limited purpose. In our society almost everyone reads; but in the ancient world literacy was rare and writing was a skill practiced by an exclusive class of scribes.

Why Writing Developed

The Bible originated in a part of the world dominated by grain production and hence large populations of the Nile Valley (Egypt) and the Tigris and Euphrates Valleys (Mesopotamia). Palestine, a hilly land dependent on rain for agriculture, was not well suited for supporting a high population. Palestine's population was therefore inclined to be comparatively low, which meant that it was easily controlled by other nations. Throughout much of its history, it was ruled over by foreign powers such as Assyria, Egypt, Babylon, Greece, and Rome. Palestine rarely if ever constituted a sovereign nation. Its kings ruled only as clients of the empire that controlled Palestine at a particular time. An example known to most of us, from about a thousand years after the time the Bible was first begun, is the Herods: they ruled Palestine on behalf of the Roman emperors.

The population of Palestine was divided into a large lower class and a small ruling class. The masses were illiterate village people who tilled the arable land. Their rulers were based in fortress cities that were more the size of compounds than anything we would call a city today. Typically the power exercised by the ruling class was guaranteed by the empire that dominated, or threatened to dominate, Palestine at the time. In the period when the earliest biblical stories were composed, this was the pharaoh in Egypt.

Writing developed a very long time ago, in both Egypt and Mesopotamia, but in its early days it was a complex art requiring the knowledge of a large number of signs and mastered only by a few. Not surprisingly, it was first developed for the purposes of taxation. In addition to being useful for record keeping and defining ownership, it also served a political purpose.

With the dawn of the ancient alphabet, writing was greatly simplified and therefore came into wider use. Rulers increasingly utilized their scribes to influence the course of events, shaping traditions previously passed down by word of mouth to further their own political ambitions.

Ordinary individuals three thousand years ago were not free to decide their own identity and chart their own destiny, as are so many of us in the modern world. Rulers spoke for the masses of the rural populace, determining what role the common folk should play in the nation's structure. They conceived of the peasants' identity for them, deciding how their world should be, and fixed their position in that world in written traditions. In a nutshell, the earliest books of the Bible arose not among common folk but in the nation's royal courts.

More Than One Story

When Israel came into existence it was not what we know as a nation. Nations as we know them did not exist. In its earliest days Israel was not organized under a single ruler. Not until the time of David did Israel become a centrally organized government. This was at a period when Egyptian power was waning. For a brief window of about sixty years, Palestine shook loose of the pharaohs' rule and became a sovereign state. This was under the kingship of David and his son Solomon.

For a long time it was thought by a majority of scholars that Solomon's reign was the background for the composition of the original document that purports to tell Israel's early history. Recently an earlier dating of the document to the reign of David has been proposed. It is suggested that it dates from around 960 B.C.E. and that it was composed in the court of David to aid in shaping the population of Palestine into an independent power.*

The story that forms the basis of the first part of the Bible contains many of the Bible's best-known stories. It begins with the second of the two creation stories, Genesis 2, continuing with Cain and Abel, Noah and the Flood, the Tower of Babel, large parts of the stories of Abram, Isaac, Jacob, and Joseph, the story of the Exodus, and culminates in the incident of Balaam's talking ass. These stories make up what is in effect the founding charter of ancient Israel.

Not all of the stories in this part of the Bible were part of the original Bible story. Some of them were added much later. For instance, in the original story Abram left Mesopotamia and journeyed to Palestine. While he was in Palestine there was a famine, so he moved to Egypt. Because his wife was beautiful, he was afraid that she might be taken into the pharaoh's harem and that he might be killed, so he told her to say that she was his sister. God then afflicted pharaoh's household with plagues, until pharaoh connected the plagues with the arrival of Sarah into his harem and approached Abram about the matter. When Abram's lie was discovered, he and his wife left Egypt laden down with wealth bestowed upon them by pharaoh.

Not long afterwards, as the Bible as we now have it reads, Abram repeated this lie to another ruler, a king in the Negeb named Abimelech. Believing Sarah to be Abram's sister, Abi-

---

The Bible's First History, Robert B. Coote & David Robert Ord (Philadelphia: Fortress Press, 1989).

melech took her to make her his wife. But God appeared to Abimelech in a dream and told him that the woman was married, whereupon Abimelech restored Sarah to Abram. As with pharaoh, Abimelech gave Abram considerable wealth.

Is it not strange that a man who feared God used the same strategy twice, bringing great suffering upon other people? Was Abram just a slow learner? Such is of course possible. But when we note that Abram's response to being found out in the second incident shows no traces of having been caught in the same lie a second time, we begin to wonder whether, like the two creation stories of Genesis, these two stories came from the pens of separate writers. Perhaps they drew on a common tradition that had been preserved in two different forms, or perhaps the second crafted his story on the basis of the first's story.

It is just such remarkable similarities between these and other stories that led scholars to the conclusion that the Torah is a composite of four different lengthy narratives. On the basis of their analysis of the text, those scholars who developed what has come to be known as the Documentary Hypothesis suggested that the first five books of the Bible, which purport to tell the history of the people of Israel, were written not all at one time by Moses but probably in at least four stages over a period of over four hundred years. These stages are labeled J, E, D, and P.

The Original Bible Story

The original Bible story, embedded in Genesis, Exodus, and Numbers, is distinguishable for the most part by its characteristic style, terminology, and subject matter. Like most ancient works it had no title, and no one knows who wrote it except that it was produced by a scribe of the royal court. It is usually referred to simply as J, the first letter of the name of God used in this story. In Germany, where J was first analyzed, that name is spelled *Jahweh*, whereas in the United States we use the anglicized version *Yahweh*.

J, then, is what scholars call both the original Bible story and the unknown scribe who wrote it. It stands for both the story and its author.

Although much of J reflects inventive imagination, its writer by no means made up the entire story. It is based on sources and traditions similar to those in many other ancient agrarian societies. The stories of creation and the Flood were imitated from similar stories found in documents from other courts in the ancient Near East. The bulk of J consists of traditions of tent-dwelling tribal sheepherders living near and within the Egyptian border with Palestine. Similar peoples in more recent periods were often known as bedouin.

We have seen that most of the subjects of David and Solomon's kingdom were not tent-dwelling sheepherders. They were peasant farmers who tilled the land, and they lived in villages rather than tents. Why then did the scribe who wrote J focus on the traditions of such sheepherders rather than on the traditions of the peasants who comprised eighty-five percent or more of the population of David's Israel? For two reasons.

First, it is likely that the overlords who ruled the peasant population of the house of David saw themselves as descendants of the powerful sheepherders thought to have ruled in the mountains of Palestine in the century or two prior to David. Their traditions talked about bedouin sheikhs the likes of Abram, Isaac, Jacob, Joseph, and Moses. Although J presents Abram, Isaac, and Jacob as Israel's ancestors stretching back centuries before the house of David came to power, in reality, if not in name, they were the sheikhs of David's time. They were contemporaneous with David.

Abram, Isaac, and Jacob were real people by another name, much like Huckleberry Finn and Tom Sawyer represent types of people who really existed but who did not necessarily have these names. Earlier lords of Israel might even have had these names. But the stories about these great sheikhs are either similar to folklore about comparable heroes in other societies or composed by the writer of J.

J's stories are about these people because they were the ruling class of the house of David. The stories were constructed to indicate how David desired these people to act with regard to the new state that he was in process of creating. If David's court desired a particular sheikh to act in a certain manner, David did not address the matter directly. Instead, David's scribe addressed the issue through the example of fictionalized ancestors. If a sheikh's ancestors behaved in such a manner, so should he. Since the scribes were the only ones who could write, they had the power to fix traditions about the ancestors in this way.

The second reason J focused on sheepherders is that David came to the throne by gradually conquering territory in southern Palestine that had been under the control of powerful sheepherders like the Israelite patriarchs described in J. These sheepherders lived mainly in the margins of Palestine, occupying the borders and acting as a barrier between Israel and Egypt. David's strength came from forming alliances with these sheikhs, alliances which were designed to buffer his kingdom against incursions from Egyptian rulers similar to pharaoh in J's story of the Exodus.

Israel's Founding Charter

The story J tells functioned for David's Israel much like the story of the Pilgrim Fathers does for modern citizens of the United States. The heart of the story is the Exodus. In this great fictionalized epic, Israel is delivered from the control of the pharaoh in Egypt. David portrayed his Israelite state as the home of the free, the land of promise, much as America has been for people in modern times. Though few Americans came to these shores with the pilgrims, in a sense all of us came here on the Mayflower. We may have come on a 747, or aboard an ocean liner, or across the Mexican or Canadian borders; but the pressure on all of us is to own the story of the Pilgrim Fathers and the Mayflower, and the symbol of the Statue of Liberty, as our own. We are supposed to draw our sense of identity from what these represent.

The Exodus is an ancient Pilgrim Fathers' story. In reality most of the populace of Palestine had never been anywhere near Egypt. They were peasants who had never been anywhere in their lives. But they identified with this story of liberation from

Egyptian tyranny because under David's monarchy Egypt no longer held sway over their lives.

The story as told in the book of Exodus has taken on epic proportions. It is portrayed as a single event that happened to the whole nation of Israel. In that sense it resembles *Animal Farm*: an exodus of several hundred thousand people never happened, any more than animals actually talked. But it is true that the small part of the Palestinian population who were sheepherders regularly wandered into the Negeb to graze flocks and sometimes found themselves entrapped into labor for the Egyptian pharaoh. Such forages into Egyptian territory are recorded in the annals of history as regular events. Often those who became entrapped might escape, and this pattern of entrapment and escape became the basis of the Exodus epic.

The grandiose story composed by David's scribes served to unite the peoples of Palestine, until this time very disunited, against a common enemy, Egypt. It was written to create a sense of national cohesion for the fledgling Israelite state, which was constantly under threat from Egypt. David used the idea that they could escape pharaoh's control and throw off Egyptian rule to galvanize different chieftains into a united state. David was the first real ruler of a Palestine-wide "Israel." His son Solomon built the temple that served for many centuries as the royal dynastic chapel of the new state.

11.

What Archaeology Reveals

In recent years the archaeologist's spade has brought to light numerous ancient creation stories. These stories illuminate the meaning of the story of Adam and Eve in the Garden of Eden.

While purporting to tell how humans were created, these stories served to keep the masses in their place, as can be seen from one such story, the Mesopotamian *Enuma Elish,* which predates the Genesis garden story by at least six hundred years. In this account of creation, before humans came into being there were only gods. The gods were like bees: there were queen bees, and there were worker bees. Some gods ruled while the rest did all the work.

In the course of time the worker gods became rowdy and threatened to disrupt the status quo. Once he had created the world, Marduk, champion of the gods, heard that the gods were complaining about all the work they had and devised an ingenious plan which he conveyed to the king of the gods, Ea: "Blood will I form and cause bone to be, then I will make humans. Upon the humans shall the services of the gods be imposed." Humans were created to do the sweaty labor formerly required of the lesser gods, in order that all the gods might enjoy a life of ease, as everyone knows gods are supposed to.

Ea suggested to Marduk that the humans be created out of the god who fomented the labor dispute. Marduk assembled the worker gods and asked them to deliver up the one who created the strife. The gods turned over the ringleader of the rebellion, who was cut up so that a new set of workers could be created out of him. In this creation story humans are made out of the blood of the ringleader of the workers' rebellion. That is why peasants, unlike the rulers (who are like gods), must do sweaty labor.

The story is not a quaint fairy tale but a powerful political tool for keeping the laboring peasants in their place, much like the aristocratic myth of blue blood. Throughout history the aristocracy have considered themselves a class of being superior to common humans. Until well into our own century, the British aristocracy fostered the belief that the ruling class have blue blood. The aristocracy considered it their God-given right to exploit the masses on their estates in order that they might lead a leisurely life of luxury. To have to work for one's living was considered extremely bad show for an aristocrat until quite recently. In similar fashion, the kings of ancient nations and the ruling elite of their royal courts promulgated the idea that they were gods and that peasants were mere humans created specifically to do their sweaty work. In this way power and privileges were maintained with the reduced threat of a peasant revolt.

While it was the lot of peasants to till the arable land in sweaty toil, and to give up much of their produce in taxes, fees, and fines, the work of the ruling class was the non-sweaty service of the chief god of the Babylonian state. Their work was symbolic work. Archaeologists have unearthed representations of the king doing the service of the gods. For instance, the Sumerian kings had themselves modeled in clay bearing the worker's basket of dirt. These kings didn't actually work, but just symbolized work. They did ceremonial work such as ground-breaking. The success of the king as the preeminent gardener of the realm was deemed crucial to the productivity of the state's entire agricultural system. If the king's garden did well, the nation's gardens prospered. But the king's role was to represent agricultural workers, not actually to do sweaty labor.

British television was privileged some years ago to take a walk with Queen Elizabeth II through the expansive private gardens that lie behind Buckingham Palace. The queen was shown nipping off an occasional bud, potting the odd plant or two, and instructing her gardeners. Nothing to generate sweat, you understand. No heavy shoveling, no wheelbarrowing, no raking of leaves for hours on end. Ancient Mesopotamian friezes likewise depict the king strolling through his realm, dropping a little fertilizer here, pruning a branch there. It's symbolic work.

What the "Garden of Eden" Is All About

J's story of the Garden of Eden responds to other creation stories of the time, contradicting their view of humanity as divided into two classes of being, rulers and workers. The narrative begins when Yahweh, a god, created the earth and the sky. Like many other translations, the New Revised Standard Version uses the expression "the Lord God," which is extremely misleading. It is important to retain the Hebrew "Yahweh, a god" because it focuses attention on the distinction between gods and humans, raising the issue of what are the privileges of gods and what is the lot of humans.

The first prerogative of gods portrayed by the story is that of creating human beings. This is strictly a divine prerogative. The god Yahweh formed a human from dirt, shaping moist clay like a potter. This creature he intended to be his worker, the one who would perform mild tasks of tending his garden.

The next thing Yahweh did was to plant a formal pleasure orchard of perennials, of the kind described in ancient literature as surrounding royal palaces. The Garden of Eden is not just any garden, but the private, enclosed formal garden, whose entrance was narrow enough to be blocked by a flashing sword (rather like a modern guarded gate house on a wealthy estate), belonging to an urban elite ruler. The garden is analogous to a meticulously pruned baroque French garden. The garden is irrigated by rivers and intensively farmed with perennials. The Garden of Eden is the symbolic royal garden that serves as the pattern for the whole realm. The word "eden" implies "pleasure" and carries sexual connotations connected with the fertility of the land and the fertility of the royal dynasty. There were many "edens" around royal palaces in the ancient world.

The human was placed in the garden to work it. The story makes it clear this is not hard labor. The New Revised Standard

Version is quite in error in Genesis 2:15 when it renders the Hebrew *avad,* meaning "work," as "till." This is an entirely different concept from "till" in Genesis 2:5, which refers to the hard, sweaty labor required to till the arable. The human whom Yahweh placed in his garden did not at first sweat in the open fields of the arable land; that came only after he was driven from the garden. He started off tending a garden of perennials in a manner that did not require sweaty toil. Adam is a royal personage, son of a god, who strolls through the garden plucking the fruit, tending to a little pruning, but nothing too strenuous — nothing to generate sweat.

The human is also required to "keep" the garden. This word has frequently been interpreted in the light of the Protestant work ethic, in the sense of upkeep; but the Hebrew *shamar* means to guard. The word implies that inside the garden is civilized, with the threat of a lack of order outside the walled enclosure. It is an oasis of royal order. In Mesopotamian literature the nature of the threat to order is clear: peasants in the surrounding countryside must be taught to maintain their orderly work routines and not join those rebels who threaten the system. We are reminded of the tale of Robin Hood, in which the Sheriff of Nottingham sallies forth from his walled city, raiding the crops of peasants who tilled the land and terrorizing them lest they organize and become a threat.

Present in the pleasure orchard was a serpent. This creature informed Adam and Eve that they could be like gods. All they had to do was eat a particular fruit that Yahweh had forbidden them to eat, a fruit that would give them the capacity to "know" — the ability to be self-aware in the way that humans are uniquely self-aware, with a sense of time and meaning, unlike any animal. When Adam and Eve took the forbidden fruit, they realized for the first time that they were sexual beings who could reproduce themselves like gods. They began to "know" good and evil — to see life in terms of actions with consequences.

In response to their attempt to elevate themselves to the plane of gods, Yahweh cursed them. Until now labor had been painless; now it would be burdensome and painful. The curse of the woman was to labor in producing human beings through painful childbirth. The curse of the man was to labor producing food from the arable outside the royal garden by the sweaty toil of tillage. Gone were the days of royal resting in the heat of the day and getting up in the cool of the evening breeze to stroll through the garden, prune a few branches, pluck an orange, peel and eat it with no sweat.

J's story, then, refutes the Mesopotamian belief that some are created to sweat while others do the symbolic work of gods. Under the curse, those who have lived like gods are evicted from their pleasure gardens and must share in the sweating. The story denies any inherent difference between ruler and ruled. In line with the tribal ethos of early Israel, it sees the people of David's Israel as sisters and brothers, not separate castes. The sweaty, painful work assigned humans when they were ejected from the royal garden is for all to share, not just for lesser beings. Yahweh intended all to be cursed with having to sweat: all must share the hard work of building David's new nation.

David's Vision for Israel

The whole of J's fictional story spans three sets of seven generations, for a total of twenty-one generations, from creation until the tribes of Israel were poised to invade Palestine. The twenty-second generation is to inherit the land of Palestine.

In the first two sets of generations, human beings continually usurp for themselves prerogatives that belong to the god Yahweh. Through fourteen generations the god responds by cursing. In the third set of generations, Yahweh tries a different way of responding to humans: he blesses. The seven generations of blessing reverse the curses of the first fourteen generations. All of the ways in which humans usurped divine privileges and were cursed are overturned by Yahweh, so that the blessed people of Israel prosper at Yahweh's hand. By the time of the twenty-second generation, when it comes time to inherit Palestine, blessing prevails over curse. The message is that those who identify with David's Israel will be blessed.

For the first two sets of generations, curse follows curse. Every time humans take to themselves a royal prerogative, Yahweh curses. Not until the fifteenth generation and the start of

the final set of generations does blessing enter, in the time of
Abram. Abram's descendants are to inherit the land of Palestine, the Israel of David. Beginning with Abram, through a series
of incidents that parallel those that led to cursing in the first
two sets of generations, blessing replaces curse. Palestine under
David's monarchy is to be the fulfillment of the promise of blessing to Abram, the place where the cursing of humans is allevi-
ated. We will touch only on the most significant incidents to
illustrate how the curse is reversed in the era of blessing.

In the generations of cursing, Adam and Eve are put out of
the garden Yahweh planted for them, banished from the land
they enjoyed in leisure. In contrast, in the generations of blessing, a new Adam and Eve — Abram and Sarai in the fifteenth
generation — receive a land grant that will be a blessing to them
and that the text describes as a veritable "garden of Eden." For
Abram to receive this promise of land he must leave the society
in which his ancestors have reproduced and where he has inher-
ited his wealth. Instead of grasping at reproductive and economic power as did Adam and Eve, he and Sarai place the issue
of offspring and their prosperity in Yahweh's hands and leave
their ancestral home. If Abram is to prosper with a royal prosperity, it is to be at the hand of Yahweh, not through his own
efforts.

The new Adam and Eve journey into Egypt. Whereas the
original couple seized for themselves the divine prerogative of
procreation, Abram and his wife set aside their conjugal relationship and behave as brother and sister. They do not live as
husband and wife. As a result, instead of being cursed they are
blessed with wealth. They leave Egypt, in a preview of the later
exodus, loaded down with riches.

Cain and Abel were born to Eve. Cain was envious of Abel's
success with Yahweh and slew him, receiving a curse for so
doing. The incident is reversed in the generations of blessing.
On the way to Palestine a quarrel arises between Abram and
Lot, whom J terms "brothers," over grazing rights. The quarrel
parallels and reverses the earlier jealousy of Cain toward his
brother Abel. Unlike Cain, Abram does not seek his own aggran-
dizement but allows Lot to claim the extremely lush and fertile
basin — a piece of royal territory like the original Eden. As a

consequence, Yahweh reiterates the land grant to Abram, spelling out the extent of the territory he is to receive in Palestine.

Two lines develop from Adam and Eve. One will lead to Abram and the generations of blessing, culminating in David as the blessed king. The other will produce a line of evil kings culminating in the epitome of evil, the pharaoh of the Exodus, the antithesis of the benign reign David offers as king of the newly created nation of Israel. It is these lines that J traces in his lengthy genealogies. We note only a few incidents from these generations, incidents characteristic of the evil line.

In the early generations of humanity as listed by J, Lemek killed a young lad simply because he felt like doing so. Lemek is a cipher for *melek* in Hebrew, meaning "king." Ancient kings imagined they had the right to kill other humans. In the generations of blessing, this supposed prerogative of kings is reversed. This is illustrated by means of the story of Melchizedek. The message is that just kings such as David do not oppress the populace, unlike the unjust king of Egypt. Melchizedek, who appears in the generation of Abram, is king of Salem (a cipher for Jerusalem). Melchizedek is a just king. He blesses Abram and gives him a tenth of his goods.* He also acknowledges the role of the Creator of heaven and earth in Abram's victory. In contrast, the king of Sodom, an unrighteous king who has descended from the cursed line of Cain, omits any acknowledgment of the role of Yahweh. Abram will accept nothing from this king because he does not attribute his success to God. The story shows that it is the prerogative of Yahweh to bless with victory in battle and to award the spoils of war, and the blessed human being Abram recognizes this. J brings this out because David comes to the throne by usurping Saul. David is portrayed as a just king, Saul as an evil king in the style of the evil line of kings that sprang from Cain. J is anxious to show that Yahweh chooses kings, and that David has been chosen above any other contender for the throne.

At the birth of a son Eve declared, "I, like Yahweh, have

---

*The NRSV translates "Abram gave him one tenth," the traditional but erroneous interpretation. The Hebrew says simply, "He gave him a tenth," assuming that everyone knows that kings reward retainers, not vice versa.

gotten a son." Whereas Eve usurped the divine prerogative of reproducing, Sarai is barren. But in old age she becomes pregnant. It is not, however, Abram's doing. The god Yahweh is the cause of her pregnancy. (This is the sense of Genesis 18.) Isaac is born as a result of the divine prerogative of determining reproduction, not as a result of human effort. The issue of reproduction is important to J because David was not a firstborn son, and according to cultural norms therefore not rightfully heir to the throne.

Another issue to be addressed is the right of selecting a mate. One of the ways David comes to power is by arranging marriages to form alliances, and by marrying the wives of powerful rivals whom he has killed. J must justify this behavior, and he does this by means of stories about cursed and blessed marriages. In the cursed generations that preceded the great Flood, men chose wives according to their own desires. From these unions giants were born, men who "made a name for themselves." This led to the great downpour that we call the Flood, when God washed the earth of the blood spilled by these self-seeking, power-hungry individuals who would stop at nothing to promote their own greatness. In contrast, in the blessed generations, when it comes time to select a wife for Isaac, Abram does not make the choice for his son but commits it to God. It is Yahweh who chooses Rebecca for Isaac. Abram and his descendants do not make a name for themselves but rely on Yahweh to make them great. Through these stories J is saying that David's marriages are not like those of the cursed kings; rather, David is blessed with wives by Yahweh in the tradition of Isaac.

Then comes the destruction of the cities of Sodom and Gomorrah. This parallels the destruction caused by the Flood. After the Flood, the descendants of the cursed line of Cain built a great tower, the tower of Babel. Scripture refers to it in Hebrew as the "city tower," or "towering city." In the ancient world there were many such "towering cities." They were the seats of royal power, religiously and in terms of reproductive, political, and economic power. Housing a dynastic temple, a palace, and grain storage facilities, they were houses of the god of a particular city or state. In the generations of cursing, Yahweh scatters such pretenses at royal power by confusing the language of the people who are building this "tower" or, in its exact meaning, "big one."

In contrast, when Lot flees from the destruction of Sodom, he escapes to a city that Scripture calls a "little one" (Zoar). Although Solomon later built a temple, the religious center of David's Israel was located in a tent called a tabernacle, like that belonging to a great sheikh, not in a dynastic temple.

Following the great Flood, Noah planted a vineyard and became drunk. While he was drunk, Noah's son committed what J regarded as an immoral act with him. Noah "knew" what Ham had done to him, and another era of cursing ensued. The theme of knowing has been important from the beginning of J's epic, being sounded first in the Garden of Eden when Adam and Eve began to "know." But human knowing will not always be cursed: in the generations of blessing, the curse is reversed by an incident that parallels that of Noah. Following the destruction of the cities of the plain, Lot like Noah becomes drunk. His two daughters go to bed with him and become pregnant. Lot does *not* "know" that his two daughters slept with him during his drunken stupor and have become impregnated by him. It seems that people in the generations of blessing can do no wrong, for instead of being cursed his daughters are blessed with progeny. The theme of blessing in the act of knowing legitimates the many sexual maneuvers by which David was helped to come to power.

The story proceeds through the generations of Jacob and of Judah and Joseph to tell how the blessed people become trapped in Egyptian labor. It lingers on Judah because David's throne is rooted in the territory and tribe of Judah. Pharaoh of Egypt is a descendant of Cain, who murdered Abel, through Noah's son Ham. Pharaoh belongs to the cursed line. Eventually Yahweh acts through Moses to deliver the sheepherders of Palestine from the pharaoh. In killing the firstborn of Pharaoh and all the firstborn of Egypt, Yahweh is requiting the murder of Abel, the firstborn of Adam and Eve. Indeed, throughout J's story Yahweh is repeatedly shown to be against firstborn sons, except his own "son" Israel, choosing lesser-born sons on whom to bestow honor. This theme is used to justify David's usurpation of the throne, since he was not a firstborn son. J's point is that it is not by right of kinship and inheritance that David's Israel prospers, but as a direct result of Yahweh's blessing.

The story traces the journey of the children of Israel through the desert toward Palestine, employing numerous incidents to establish the authority of a single ruler in the person of Moses. The note that is being sounded is that Palestine is no longer to be ruled over by many leaders, but that all should give their allegiance to a single central authority, Yahweh's one true king, David. Moses is, quite simply, a figure who stands for David, the one who in David's stead promulgates Israel's law.

J's narrative culminates in the encounter of the blessed people with Balaam. The sheepherders are poised to enter Palestine, having left Egypt behind. A king hires Balaam, a prophet, to curse these people. But this is the era of blessing, and these are the blessed people. The curse can no longer triumph against blessing. There are only two talking animals in the Bible. The first was the snake in the garden, in an incident that led to cursing. In this final incident in J's story, it is Balaam's ass that talks. Balaam is forbidden to curse Israel. Paid to curse, Balaam is able only to bless.

J's story invites the powerful sheepherding sheikhs of David's time to follow in the steps of their fictionalized ancestors and join in the march of success that is David's monarchy. It invites them to participate in a centralized rule under the authority of David. Through this newly formed state, blessing will come to all the peoples of the earth. In the person of David, Yahweh has acted to end the curse and bring peace and prosperity to all.

David's vision for the new state was indeed magnificent. For a brief window of about sixty years Israel was a "free" people. But it did not last. Solomon oppressed the masses just as Pharaoh had done in Egypt. As a result, the Davidic monarchy collapsed. And that collapse led to the first major revision of J's original story.

12.

Stories of Political Intrigue

J is not the only story contained in the early books of the Bible. There are at least three other types of material, each with its own distinctive set of characteristics.

For a long time scholars thought that these different types each marked what was once a separate document, just as J was once a document in its own right, and that these separate documents were spliced together at later stages. Some historians continue to believe this to be the case, and they may be partly right. It is more likely, however, that two of these further types of material mark revisions of J, in the form of additions, while the third is a complete story in itself.

The view that the different types of material that make up the early books of the Bible were originally separate documents was formed under the influence of the romantic idea that every nation had what was basically a single repertoire of shared traditions, rooted in historical reality. According to this theory, the traditions of the nation Israel were preserved in four variant forms, and this explains why they have much in common. This is like the view that the four gospels all tell essentially the same story, since they are all supposedly rooted in the more or less accurate remembering of the historical Jesus.

This turns out to be no more the case with the early books of the Bible than, as we saw in Part I, with the four gospels. As in the case of the gospels, what is really interesting about these separate strands of material in the early books of the Bible is what they do not have in common, rather than what they do. What they have in common can easily be explained by assuming that each succeeding set of additions took what was already there more or less for granted. What they do not have in common must be understood on the basis of their different points of view, based on the different contexts they represent. This can be illustrated by looking at two of the three remaining types of material.

In Defense of a Revolt

A second set of texts, all found in Genesis and Exodus, is quite different from J. Historians call these texts E. E likes to call Yahweh simply "God," which is *Elohim* in Hebrew, hence the E. E adds to J about a dozen incidents which show how the ancestors of Israel were in critical jeopardy of their lives and were rescued in the nick of time, usually by virtue of someone's fear of God. Think of the famous story of how Abraham nearly sacrificed Isaac. That is a typical E story.

E took a particular interest in the story of one ancestor in jeopardy, Joseph. Why was E interested in Joseph? E was probably written in the court of Jeroboam I who, after Solomon's death, led the North in a rebellion against the house of David. Israel split into two kingdoms, known as Israel and Judah (sometimes called the house of David). Jeroboam, the first king of Israel, opposed to the house of David, felt it necessary to justify his secession, and E was written for this purpose. It dates from about forty years later than J, around 920 B.C.E.

Jeroboam belonged to the tribe tracing its lineage to Joseph, just as David traced his ancestry to Judah. Joseph appears in J, but there he is not the focus of the action. J's story of Joseph centers on Judah. Joseph was persecuted by the rest of his brothers, who sold him as a slave into Egypt. J's story emphasizes that it was Judah who was decisively instrumental in reconciling Joseph with the brothers. The story addresses how the northern hill country, or Joseph, was to be integrated into the new state headed by Judah. Joseph represents this mountain land. What is at issue is the unity of the tribes of Israel under David. Will the ruler from Judah prevail or the ruler from the northern hill country? J's intent is to point to David, the descendant of Judah, as the cohesive force among the tribes of Israel. It is David who binds them together as a single nation.

E has a different purpose altogether. Through E's additions, the story of Joseph as we know it was created. Throughout his work E made use of dreams to get his message over. This he does extensively in the Joseph story, adding a series of dreams to J's earlier story of Joseph in Egypt. Joseph has dreams, Pharaoh's butler and chief baker have dreams, and Pharaoh himself has dreams. None of these dreams were part of J's original story. Through these dreams E enables Joseph to become the center of the drama, eclipsing Judah.

In the first dream, a dream which Joseph himself had when he was seventeen years old, the twelve sons of Jacob were binding sheaves in the field. Joseph's sheaf arose and stood upright, and the brothers' sheaves gathered around it and bowed down to his sheaf. When Joseph told the dream to his brothers, they responded, "Are you indeed to reign over us? Or are you indeed to have dominion over us?" (Gen 37:8). In the second dream, the sun, the moon, and eleven stars bowed down to Joseph. When he told the dream to his family, his father responded, "Shall I and your mother and your brothers indeed come to bow ourselves to the ground before you?" The dreams point to Joseph's greatness in Egypt — and to Jeroboam's rule over Israel in Palestine.

The northern hill country had a perennial tendency toward independence from the rule of Jerusalem. This part of Palestine had long been prone to make separate alliances with the great powers of the Middle East such as Egypt. E's story of how Joseph became great in Egypt takes this tendency a step further. Joseph's greatness in Egypt foreshadows northern Israel's revolt against Judah, and Jeroboam's declaration of the northern territory as an independent kingdom. In E's story Pharaoh is the one who makes Joseph ruler: he governs with the permission and backing of the Egyptian king. Jeroboam was in fact an Egyptian client. The northern territory that became the kingdom of Israel could not have split off from the southern kingdom of Judah without the support of Egypt.

Why was E added to J? It is likely that a scribe under Jeroboam added E to J in order to adopt an "official" history of Israel for Jeroboam's court, since Jeroboam now claimed to be the legitimate king of Israel, and to adapt it to reflect some concerns of Jeroboam's court. These included the apparent danger to Jeroboam's sons, one of whom he hoped would succeed him. At least one son fell ill and died prematurely, and it is likely that at least one other was held hostage in Egypt, just like Simeon (and potentially Benjamin) in E's story of the brothers' visit to Egypt to buy grain in a time of famine.

Most of E concerns the court of Jeroboam. Although Jeroboam adopted the house of David's history of Israel, Jeroboam's rule was founded on his opposition to the house of David. Thus it makes no more sense for us to read J and E together, as though they had come from the same national tradition or had always expressed the same point of view, than it does to read the four gospels as if they had a common origin and point of view. Just as each gospel must be read for its own unique message, so should J and E be understood as conveying very different points of view.

How We Got the Most Famous of All Creation Stories

The third set of writings found in the early books of the Bible brings us back to the creation story with which the Bible opens in Genesis 1. This creation story stands at the head of what scholars refer to as the priestly strand, or P. It dates from some four centuries later than J and E.

We have seen that complex writing of the sort we have in the Scriptures was in the ancient world limited to a scribal class who flourished in connection with urban palaces and temples. Creation stories in the ancient Near East emanated from these temples. In the minds of rulers and the aristocracy, the temple was conceived of as the palace of the god (which is why in Hebrew terms like "house" and "palace" are used for temple). The nation's temple was the cornerstone of creation, the center of the world produced by the god, the place where the god met with humans to issue laws.

In the thinking of the ancients, the earth was originally sea. The order that is seen on land in nature emerged out of the chaos of the sea. As the land is an island of order in a sea of chaos, so was the urban palace-temple complex a haven of order in the midst of the sea of potentially lawless peasants who worked the land outside the cities. The temple epitomized the order seen in creation, and it was from such temples that laws to establish order in society were promulgated.

In ancient creation stories the god creates the common mass of humanity to do work and service in the world, in place of the gods, who, like the ruling class, avoid the kind of dirt work undertaken by peasants, dwelling instead in their palaces and temples, devoting themselves to their main activities: military expeditions for the royal class, and butchery and clerical work for the priestly class. The priests served the god in his house. As the god's representatives, they ate the meat of the god. The animals created were the main fare of the priests, brought to the temple as sacrifices. It was the privilege of the priesthood to eat meat, a luxury, in abundance.

P's focus is a lengthy set of instructions regarding the Tabernacle and its worship, its utensils, priests, and the blood taboos and other laws laid down at its shrine. In J, now supplemented by E, the brief law promulgated at Sinai was chiefly law regarding how the people were to worship their god. The priestly writer could use this slot in the history, beginning in Exodus 25, to insert his main subject, a grand elaboration of the laws of the official Judahite cult. P is found mainly in Exodus 25-40, Leviticus, and a large part of Numbers, but also includes a good deal of narrative supplementation in Genesis and Exodus. The creation story in Genesis 1 provides a conceptual foundation for the idea of Israel as a people who belonged to and were meant to serve the god.

The set on which Genesis 1 opens is a world that lacks order. God issues ten successive commands that bring order out of chaos. The world of nature is obedient. The priestly writer was preoccupied with obedience. When disobedience occurs, reparations must be made. This is the basic purpose of the "sacrifices," or meat meals, that are the focus of the work of the priesthood.

Order emerges out of chaos over a period of six days. On the first day God creates light. The light is separated from darkness, marking out each period of twenty-four hours with night and day. All that God has made so far are the realms of light and dark; the heavenly bodies that move in these realms—the sun, moon, and stars—will not be created until the fourth day. To our minds, such a view of creation is absurd. But this is not a scientific understanding of the cosmos. All that the priestly writer was concerned with was establishing order by separating everything into its proper place.

On the second day God creates the firmament—a translucent dome that separates the upper waters from the seas. Recall that in the view of the ancients the heavens were not space but water. So now God has created the realms of sky and sea. The creatures that move in sky and sea will not be created until day five.

On the third day God creates dry land and vegetation. Again, all that God has created so far is the realms of land and vegetation. No animals or humans will appear on the scene to occupy the land or eat the vegetation until the sixth day.

What has emerged is a pattern of two sets of days, each consisting of three days. During the first three days God creates the realms, which are fixed in place. During the second three days God creates the bodies that move within each of the realms. Hence on Day 4, which parallels Day 1, heavenly bodies such as sun, moon, and stars come into being to move in the realms of light and dark. On Day 5, which parallels Day 2, birds and fish come into being to move in the realms of sky and sea. And on Day 6, animals and humans are created to move in and use the realms of land and vegetation. It is a world that is perfectly ordered, with everything beautifully separated, each category of moving object designated to move in its appropriate realm. All moving creatures are ordered to eat only vegetation, not other creatures.

How the creation story of Genesis 1 formed an ideological basis for the priestly cult may be seen from the laws governing what may or may not be eaten. It is on the basis of the separation of creatures into their appropriate realms, as well as the classification of how the moving creatures actually do move and whether they eat only vegetation, that the laws of purity concerning animals fit for food are based. Leviticus 11 distinguishes between creatures that are edible and creatures that are inedible. Whether a creature may be eaten depends on whether it fits the definition of what is normative for a creature that belongs to that realm. The ideal type of animal suited for the land has cloven hooves (no claws for attacking other creatures) and chews the cud (vegetation chewed again and again). The ideal type of sea creature has fins and scales, not legs and skin like a land creature. The ideal type of flying creature is less precisely spelled out but may be discerned from the characteristics of the creatures listed as edible or taboo. Creatures of the sky must have wings and not eat other creatures.

Essentially there is a proper way to move within a realm: cloven hooves for land, fins for water, and wings for sky. Those creatures that fit into more than one realm, or do not conform to the ideal for a particular realm, are disorderly and may not be eaten. Thus crabs, shrimp, octopus, eels and rays may not be eaten because they either walk or snake through water. Birds like the ostrich, or birds that float in the water (even though they also fly), are excluded because they are not strictly "birds of the air." Flying insects are also excluded because they both fly and walk around on legs. On the other hand, grasshoppers, locusts, and crickets are edible because they hop, which the priests regarded as a form of flight. (But note that those who composed the laws of Deuteronomy disagreed with this last category, making such hopping insects unclean: Deut 14).

Along with the many laws of purity, the priestly writer's other major addition to J and E was to introduce a sequence of covenants. P modifies JE's scheme of generations to place three eternal covenants in the time of Noah, Abraham, and Moses. They are called eternal covenants to signify their extreme importance. Each covenant is marked by a sign: first the rainbow (Genesis 9), then circumcision (Genesis 17), and then the sabbath (Exodus 31), as well as by a particular term when speaking of or to God.

When was P written? Babylon invaded Judah and in 598 B.C.E. deported the bulk of the house of David, including the priests, and put their own puppet on the Davidic throne. Eleven years later they destroyed the temple. But late in the same century, under Persian sponsorship, the temple was rebuilt and the priesthood reinstated. A common view is that P reflects the temple as it was known in the time of the kings of Judah in Jerusalem, but that in its present form it represents the partly disenfranchised priesthood of the house of David in exile or early in the Persian period in Palestine, perhaps just before the temple was rebuilt.

The sacrificial temple worship of the house of David was never the center of life of more than a tiny minority of Palestinians under Davidic rule, but it clearly is the center of P, and therefore of the first four books of the Bible as we now know them.

The Rest of the Old Testament

As it turns out, the picture of a significant portion of the Bible being built up gradually by the process of supplementation applies to most of the rest of the Bible.

In the Old Testament, in addition to J and its supplements by E and P, there were narratives from the early days of the Davidic dynasty, written probably in the time of David himself, which became the basis of the next seven books of the Bible: Deuteronomy through 2 Kings (leaving aside Ruth, which, although it appears in this section in our English Bible, was written much later). This monumental work dates almost entirely from before the time of the exile, and therefore preceded the writing of P. In its completed form, it comes mainly from the time of King Josiah of Judah.

In 722 B.C.E. the Assyrians conquered the northern kingdom of Israel, and a few years later wrested control of the Davidic kingdom to the south. But by the middle of the next century, Assyrian power began to wane. King Josiah of Judah, seeing the decline of Assyria, seized the opportunity to expand his kingdom. He set out to restore the house of David to the former glory of Solomon's kingdom, not only in Judah but elsewhere in Israelite Palestine.

To foster this nationalistic revival, Josiah instituted a revival of the state religion. Religion and political revival often go hand-in-hand. The worship conducted in the temple, the focus of the house of David's power, became of supreme importance. In connection with this temple, Josiah had a great law collection and history compiled, known as the Deuteronomistic History. It represents a sophisticated amalgam of Moses and David traditions. Like J in an earlier period of Israelite history, it served as a charter document, the basis of the revitalized state of Israel. Just as J used the fictionalized character of Moses to portray the rule of David, so Josiah's scribe created the character of Joshua as a model for Josiah. The territory Joshua is spoken of as conquering becomes the territory that Josiah envisions as his revived Israelite empire. The books of Deuteronomy through 2 Kings, referred to by scholars as the Deuteronomistic History, or D, are Josiah's visionary work, in the form of a law collection and history. They comprise a single lengthy document. Although the scribe who composed D also revised parts of the combined work of JEP, D's main story is not a revision or supplementation of J but is in itself a complete story.

The end result of this process of composition and recomposition that began with David, continued in the court of Jeroboam I, in the court of Josiah, and with the priests of the time of the Babylonian exile, is known to us as the Pentateuch and Former Prophets, or the books of Genesis through 2 Kings. There were many stages of composition along the way, and the whole process spanned 450 years or more. Many different viewpoints are expressed in this section of the Bible, reflecting the reality that much changes, even in one place and under one regime, in such a span of time.

The books of Chronicles are a further revision of everything between Genesis and 2 Kings, a revision carried out to reflect the circumstances of Jerusalem in the Persian period. Ezra and Nehemiah come from the same time. The poetic, reflective, and instructional books that follow in the English Bible come from the same lengthy span of years. All of them except for possibly the Song of Songs show internal development—in the case of the Psalms, over a thousand years. Within Psalms there are many reflections of other parts of the Bible, as in the headings like that to Psalm 51. Proverbs may have taken nearly as long to emerge in its present form. Job was written in only two basic stages, though the main poetic narrative is of a very ancient type of which much older examples are known.

The prophetic books are all composites, possibly excepting Ezekiel. Isaiah represents at least four significant stages and points of view, written between about 730 and 430 B.C.E. Each succeeding stage made use of the earlier stages, giving the book a wonderful metaphorical coherence, despite its stylistic variations. Jeremiah was probably written over a period of at least 75 years, beginning within the lifetime of the prophet for which it is named. It makes many allusions to Scriptures already existing, including JEP and Hosea. The twelve shorter prophetic books (not including Daniel, which was written in the second century B.C.E., making it the latest book in the Old Testament) were gathered together by stages over time, and some of them show at least three stages of composition themselves. Amos was written in at least three stages, just like Isaiah or JEP, and the combination of Joel, Amos, Obadiah, and Jonah belongs together as a single unit in which one part refers to another in remarkable ways.

How We Got the New Testament

The English Christian Bible is organized in such a way that the last book before the New Testament is Malachi, which is referred to at the beginning of the gospels in a significant way. Speaking on behalf of God, Malachi says, in words popularized by Handel's *Messiah:*

> Behold, I send my messenger to prepare the way before me, and the Lord whom you seek will suddenly come to his temple; the messenger of the covenant in whom you delight, behold, he is coming, says the Lord of hosts . . . Behold, I will send you Elijah the prophet before the great and terrible day of the Lord comes.

Malachi's reference to the coming of Elijah and the Lord to the temple is one of the three scriptural bases of Mark's story of Jesus. The others are the story of the Exodus, originally from

J, and the whole book of Isaiah, especially its metaphor of the "servant" of the Lord. Mark was written to make sense of the lordship of Christ in light of the changing circumstances toward the end of the first century C.E.

Mark's synthesis of principal Old Testament themes with Jesus as the Christ was so significant, yet in some ways inadequate, that at least two, and possibly all three, of the other gospels were revisions of it. This is most obvious in the case of Matthew, which contains nearly the whole of Mark.

Matthew uses more than 600 of Mark's 661 verses, interspersed with other material so that the gospel is nearly twice as long as Mark's original.

The process whereby four gospels came into being is identical to that which gave us most of the Old Testament. Mark is to J as Matthew is to J and E together. Matthew was written because Mark makes it appear that Jesus had no use for the Torah, the Jewish law as enshrined in the books of Moses, the first five books of the Bible. The writer of Matthew regarded this as an unfortunate and undesirable implication of Mark and set out to revise this impression. Matthew's Gospel is divided into five major sections, a reflection of the five books of the law. Matthew's Jesus gives a new law based wholly on the Torah; this law is found in the Sermon on the Mount, which is equivalent to Mount Sinai where Moses delivered the original law. Even though Matthew otherwise has some extremely critical things to say about the Pharisees, he insists that followers should do exactly what the Pharisees say since they "sit in the seat of Moses."

Luke and Acts constitute a single work in two parts. Like Matthew, Luke's work is a revision of Mark, possibly with an awareness of Matthew. Its intent is to incorporate the work and teachings of Paul, whose letters became increasingly important toward the end of the first century but who is not mentioned in either Mark's or Matthew's Gospel. Why should he be mentioned, we might ask, since the gospel is about Jesus Christ? Yet this is precisely what Luke found inadequate about the gospel as it was available to him. For Luke, as the message of Jesus spread beyond the bounds of Palestine to Asia Minor and eventually Rome itself, different cultural contexts meant that new interpretations were necessary, built of course on the bedrock of what had come before. Paul, the newly celebrated champion of the gospel in the context of the Roman Empire, had to be made an essential part of the gospel. As the message was adapted for different societies, it had to be shown once again, for late-first-century readers and hearers, that the Christian way represented a genuine fulfillment of not only the Torah, but the Prophets in Scripture as well.

The relation between the gospels of John and Mark is less clear and much debated, but it is likely that John is indebted to Mark in significant ways, despite the major discrepancies between the two works. John's version of how Jesus relates to the Torah is expressed in cosmic, universal terms, starting with the creation of the world. This goes back much further into the past than do the Christmas accounts in Matthew or Luke. But this does not mean that John's account of Jesus is a sweeping panorama of his life and ministry. Far from it. In fact, John's horizons are actually a good deal more confined than those of the other gospels.

Not only does John not cover Jesus' birth or infancy, but also much of the public ministry described in the other gospels is absent from John. Indeed, most of the ministry is conducted in private conversations rather than through public healings and preaching—and much of this takes place indoors. John expands Jesus' ministry from a single year in the synoptic gospels to three years, but he condenses this three-year period into only a portion of his gospel, devoting himself largely to the final events of Jesus' life. The focus is on a single "hour," as John calls it—an "hour" which, as we have seen, is heralded from the beginning of the gospel.

The people for whom John speaks appear to have been excluded from the synagogue, and to be under dire threat from the Judean leaders of the synagogue in their locality. This situation produces a version of Jesus' deeds and words that is more than ever imbued with judicial process and rectitude, although John's judicial interest is almost entirely confined to his church's local conflict with their fellow Judeans. John's people are under too direct a threat from these Judeans to be overly concerned, outside of the final trial scene, with the practical and public matter of maintaining the integrity of the Judean right to have Judean magistrates, as addressed by Matthew. Neither are they concerned with making a contribution to good relations between Judeans and Rome by showing that it is not a betrayal of Judean identity to appeal to Roman magistrates, as addressed by Luke. This, along with other differences, gives the gospel of John its distinctive character, despite its debt to Mark.

Although it is a complex collection, the New Testament may thus be regarded as stemming mainly from just two basic sources, the Gospel of Mark and the letters of Paul, which were then revised, supplemented, clarified, and expanded, as the metaphors and tensive language of the Hebrew Scriptures and earlier Christian works resonated in a variety of Christian contexts. It is generally believed by scholars that seven of Paul's letters were written by Paul himself, while others were either revisions of his work or written by later individuals who belonged to or claimed to belong to the same school of thought and therefore wrote in his name. The books that find their roots in either Mark or Paul themselves consist of a dense network of references and allusions to the Scriptures and internal cross-references, which reinterpret the Scriptures as circumstances change.

A Message in Metaphors

It turns out that, even as we found the gospels to be literary works whose intent is to convey a message rather than to present a factual account of historical events, the Bible as a whole is literature that deals with meaning rather than fact. The rich type of imagery characteristic of John's Gospel extends throughout the Bible. Indeed the Bible may be said to be one long, complex skein of metaphors. Through these metaphors the biblical writers build out of words a vision of an alternative world. They create for their readers a view of the world that they want them to believe in.

These metaphors were developed, presented to the community, and adopted by the community in which they arose. Over the course of time they were adapted to the changing needs of the community, often becoming completely transformed in meaning. They were also frequently imitated. Eventually such metaphors were discarded as no longer useful, only to be recovered and recycled by later generations that once again found them meaningful.

Given that there were many, many such writings in the world of the Bible, how did precisely these writings become the authoritative books of the church? This is the question we address in the next chapter.

13.

When the Bible Became the Bible

As people who are accustomed to viewing the Bible as the source of our faith, we may long to take up a solid position in the midst of the shifting sands of writing, revising, and interpretation that produced the Bible. Not everything is shifting, we may try to assure ourselves. Some things still stand. Some pillar, some foundation, some bedrock is surely to be found.

Is there not some sense in which the Bible as *The Bible* is a solid foundation? Don't the Bible's venerable black leather covers in some way establish the beginning and the end of the Word of God? Certainly the table of contents to the Bible declares by implication that these books are what constitute the Word of God, and nothing else.

This extremely popular belief that the Bible is the Word of God assumes that there was a moment in the past when the Bible became a complete entity. At some point in history, according to this view, God made sure that what we call the biblical *canon* was intact. The word "canon" means "measure" or yardstick. It implies that all of the books were brought together at some point, furnishing us with the complete Word of God.

A Perfect Original Text?

People who seek certainty from the Bible often speak of the original inspired texts, written in Hebrew, Aramaic, and Greek.

These, they are certain, were perfect. It is assumed that the textual errors that litter every manuscript in existence by the hundreds crept in subsequent to the formation of the inspired original.

It does not seem to occur to those who take this viewpoint that we do not have a single fragment of these supposed original texts. Even if there were once upon a time perfect texts, that would do us little good in the present. Existing texts have passed through centuries of political and religious intrigue, during the course of which not only were endless scribal errors made in copying, but also deliberate alterations were introduced into the text by sometimes well-meaning individuals seeking to "clarify" the meaning — and sometimes opportunists seeking to bolster a particular viewpoint.

A classic example of altering the text to support a doctrine relates to the long centuries of debate about the nature of the Trinity. Speaking of witnesses to Jesus as the Christ, I John 5:7-8 states in the New Revised Standard Version:

> There are three that testify: the Spirit and the water and the blood, and these three agree.

This and other modern translations omit words that many took for granted for centuries in the King James Version. This version reads:

> For there are three that bear record *in heaven, the Father, the Word, and the Holy Ghost: and these three are one. And there are three that bear witness in earth,* the spirit, and the water, and the blood; and these three agree in one.

Today it is common knowledge that the italicized words had no place in the earliest manuscripts and were added by a scribe.

Why, one wonders, would God go to the trouble of ensuring a perfect text to begin with and then allow it to be tampered with in all kinds of ways over the succeeding centuries? How does a perfect text that existed only momentarily help anyone today — or for that matter, anyone for the last 1,900 years? If it was not to remain perfect, what was the point of it?

Such a view ignores the realities of how we got the Bible. At no point in history was there ever a single official text of the Bible, either in the original languages of Hebrew, Aramaic, and Greek, or in translations, except as determined by committees and scholars who disagreed with one another in many, many ways, all along the way from the biblical period until now.

Because printing did not exist, the only way any work of literature could be read by more than one person at a time was for copies to be made by hand. Literally thousands of copies were made over a course of many generations. It took quite some time to copy even a single book of the Bible. Anyone who tries copying a few pages of the Bible quickly discovers how long it would take to copy a whole book, let alone the whole Bible! The idea of copying a text accurately, without changing anything, was known and affirmed even in those centuries when it was common to doctor texts while copying them; but to judge from the manuscripts that have survived, in the biblical period itself the exact copying of texts had more to do with theory than with practice.

During most of the biblical period the group of scribes charged with copying was the same as the group of scribes charged with producing new documents of annals, explanations, rationales, catalogues, genealogies, prayers, and songs. If a ruler wanted his scribes to popularize a new idea or explanation, it was useful if it could be attached to, or made an integral part of, an already existing work. Thus the pressure was strong to revise established writings while copying them for transmission to the next generation, all the while acting as if it were the same old writing with no changes. This is much like successive drafts of a memo working its way through an organization, picking up points of view from different departments as it gets composed. If this happens in a relatively short period of time in a concise memo, imagine what happened over the course of hundreds of years in the case of the much lengthier writings that make up the Bible, as they passed through the hands of one ruler or supervisor after another, each with a point of view to push.

In the case of the Old Testament, so many variations arose in the biblical texts during the process of copying that eventually Jewish scribes under the direction of ruling rabbis in Palestine and Babylonia decided to establish a relatively standard text.

This is called the Masoretic text, a term that refers to the "tradition" as more or less fixed.

In time the original Hebrew texts were translated into Greek, Aramaic, and other languages, and these also underwent interpretive changes during the process of transmission. While historians by convention refer to the Greek translation as the Septuagint, which implies a single text, as if all manuscripts of the Greek were the same, a glance at a scholarly edition of the Greek translation of any biblical book would show the great variation in the transmission of the translation.

Who Decided Which Books Should Be in the Bible?

Not only was the text of the Bible never fixed, the biblical canon itself cannot be understood in terms of a single brief moment in time when a selection was made, signed, sealed, and delivered. There has never been one authoritative list of what is in the Bible. Even the Bible's table of contents consists of shifting sands!

Two broadly defined organizations finally decided what should be normative, or canonical, among the writings available to them, and how they should be ordered, although within each there is variation, sometimes wide. In the case of the Old Testament the organization was the rabbis. Even they had a lot of disagreement about whether Ezekiel or Esther should be included, and what the order of the Prophets should be. And many probably would have favored the inclusion of some of the books now found in the so-called Apocrypha (to be discussed in a moment), since when these became a part of the Christian Bible many Christians still thought of themselves as belonging to a Jewish organization. In the case of the New Testament it was the organization of bishops under the rule of the Roman emperors who established a standard collection. This did not happen until by and large the fourth century. There were many disagreements, especially between the Western and Eastern sectors of the church, and particularly over the question of whether the Revelation and the Shepherd of Hermes should be included. In time, however, a particular set of documents became stan-

dard, on the basis of their popularity, claims of ancient authorship, agreement with or support of official rulings and
theologies, and how well they dealt with essential issues such as
how Christians were different from Judeans who were becoming
Jews or how Christians were supposed to relate to Roman
authority.

After some measure of agreement was reached on what books
constituted authoritative Scripture, the Bible in the West was
preserved for over a thousand years by the Roman Catholic
Church. But then came a fresh wave of disagreement about the
contents of Scripture. At the time of the Protestant Reformation, in their desire to reject everything that smacked of Cathol-
icism the Reformers looked for a way to change the church's
Bible, since the Bible was to be the foundation of the reformed
church. The accepted Bible of the church had been for many
centuries the Latin Vulgate, a translation of the Hebrew, Aramaic, and Greek Scriptures. Translating the Bible into German,
French, English, and many other languages, which was done for
several good reasons, was one way the Reformers produced their
own non-Catholic Bible.

Another way was to say that since the Old Testament was
originally in Hebrew it should only contain those books that exist
in the Hebrew version. The reformers then looked to their Jewish neighbors to find out what was in the Hebrew version, mis-
takenly assuming that the Jewish version was more original, and
adopted the Jewish canon as their own Old Testament. During
the more than a thousand years that the Roman Catholics preserved the Scripture, most Christian Bibles contained not only
the books that are now found in the Protestant Old Testament
but also those found in what Protestants call the Apocrypha.
This was the Bible of the Roman Catholic church, from which
the Protestant churches by and large spring. Most Protestant
churches changed the Bible's table of contents at this time. The
Christian books not in the Jewish canon were relegated to the
category of Apocrypha, which is a Greek term meaning "hidden
(books)." So what Protestants think of as the Old Testament is
among Christians only as old as the sixteenth century.

The conflict that divided the Catholic and Protestant
churches on the contents of Scripture was a continuation of

similar disagreements that have existed within and among the communities of faith since the Bible first began to be written. Why did these communities choose some writings rather than others for inclusion among authoritative Scriptures?

The process leading to the Bible more or less as we know it took over 1,800 years, a process that was completed during the first few centuries of the church (with the exception of changes made during the Reformation). It was a lengthy and complex process of interpretation. It is necessary to look at the whole process. When we do so, we see clearly why simple notions of biblical inspiration and authority make little sense for today's church.

When Politics and Religion Mixed

To understand why the writings that are now in the Bible were written and why they were regarded as important, it is necessary to emphasize once again that in the ancient world writing was extremely limited. Lengthy literary works of the kind found in the Bible were extremely rare. The same goes for readers. Until Greek became widespread in the cities of the Near East under Roman rule, lengthy texts were produced almost entirely in rulers' courts or their shrines, like the temple in Jerusalem.

A key concern for ancient rulers was their right to rule. In Palestine, as in all ancient societies, the right to rule was contested, with no letup whatever, by rival lords and outlaws of the realm. Might was an important basis of the right to rule. But influence over the minds and sensibilities of rivals and the populace was also essential and often more cost-effective. Such influence was achieved through monumental architecture such as Solomon's temple, through elaborate ritual such as the rites of the temple, and through writing.

The Old Testament consists almost entirely of positions taken by powerful factions in political struggles. The winners in these struggles commissioned the literary works that form the Old Testament, or had existing documents revised to validate their viewpoint. These documents take the form of dynastic histories.

They offer a defense of the rule of particular political figures, support from influential prophets, a justification for locating the headquarters of the religion in the royal chapel, and rituals and laws that further the purposes of the ruler and his priestly hierarchy.

The winner who started it all was David, an outlaw who became the king of Judah in the south and then usurped the kingship of Israel in the north from Saul. This he had to have explained to himself, allies, contenders like himself, and the disenfranchised of the house of Saul. The explanation occupies I Samuel and parts of II Samuel.

David was succeeded in a disorderly manner by one of his younger sons, Solomon, who also had some explaining to do, which is also in the Bible. Solomon strengthened his position by building the temple, a grand family chapel in honor of dynastic succession.

Solomon's oppressive rule was extremely unpopular in Israel in the north. So when he died, the lords of Israel, with many of their peasant followers, rebelled against the house of David and its temple in the south. With Egyptian aid, they refounded a non-Davidic monarchy in northern Israel under Jeroboam I. It is likely that the supplement to David's national history J, called E, was added in the courts of Jeroboam I.

This series of usurpations, revolts, and refoundings of the northern monarchy continued through the reigns of Jehu and his successors, until in 722 B.C.E. northern Israel, known as Samaria, fell to the Assyrians, marking the end of the non-Davidic kingdom of Israel. In the south, Hezekiah in the eighth century B.C.E. and Josiah in the seventh century reasserted the right of the house of David to rule over the north. They stressed the primacy of the temple in Jerusalem as a source of law and order and prosperity. These claims led to the writing of most of Deuteronomy through 2 Kings in their present form (D), and to the foundation of the prophetic books.

But the house of David was not going to win forever. After Josiah, they were forced to pay tribute to Babylon. When Josiah's sons rebelled, Babylon captured Jerusalem and destroyed the temple. This occurred at the beginning of the sixth century. By the end of the sixth century, the Persians had captured Babylon.

At first the Persians seemed set to restore the house of David as a puppet regime. But while the Persians permitted the dynastic temple to be rebuilt, they ended up setting aside the dynasty itself. The temple priesthood now administered Judah, or Jehud as it was then called. Most of the rest of the Old Testament, including P, Chronicles, and much of the Psalms and Prophets, comes from this priesthood. Their writings explain their right to rule and express loyalty to their Persian overlords.

Thus the Scriptures are an accumulation of interpretations of how the Jerusalem temple started by the house of David came to power. These Scriptures served well under a succession of imperial masters, until the Romans conquered Palestine in the first century B.C.E.

In the Absence of a Temple

The Romans set up Herod the Great as their puppet ruler in Palestine. Herod relied less on the traditional priestly leaders of Judea and more on monumental architecture to justify his rule. He began rebuilding the temple on such a massive scale that it was not completed until well after his own death and the death of Jesus. But despite the grandeur of Herod's temple, the Judeans were disorderly, with various factions vying for power, with the result that in 67 C.E. the Roman legions invaded Palestine to put down a widespread Judean revolt. Jerusalem was captured in 70 C.E. and the temple was once again destroyed. As things turned out, it was never rebuilt.

The destruction of the temple in 70 C.E. was the crisis that led to the formation of the New Testament. This statement may come as something of a surprise, as one might think that the life, death, and resurrection of Jesus was what lay behind the New Testament. That, of course, is true. Only it does not explain why what is generally regarded as the earliest gospel in the New Testament, Mark, was not written until forty years after Jesus' death, why this gospel became the basis for the other canonical gospels, which found Mark inadequate but essential, or why the letters of Paul, against whom authorized leaders in the church vehemently polemicized for years, form the other basis of the

New Testament. If Mark were simply an authentic "Life of Jesus," we would expect such a document from much closer to Jesus' lifetime. But that is not what Mark is. In reality Mark is an interpretation of the life and death of Jesus in the light of the fall of Jerusalem, where the church was headquartered, and the destruction of the church's temple.

What made Mark's version of the life of Jesus so important? The destruction of the temple, where Jesus' followers themselves had worshiped, and where Jesus might be expected to return to establish his rule, meant that the basic issue of the Scriptures, the legitimacy of temple rule in the name of David, had become problematic. As the years went by and it became apparent that the disaster was permanent, a new understanding of Jesus' relation to temple rule and the temple's Scriptures had to be formulated. Mark was looked back upon as the opening move in this reformulation. In Mark, Jesus pronounces the fall of the temple himself, and this becomes one of the essential themes of the church's message for the first time. Mark also portrays Jesus as setting aside the Davidic title, a novelty that the revisers of Mark in later gospels reject as unacceptable.

With the destruction of the temple, Paul's star rose like a rocket. Unlike most early Christians, Paul had argued that the temple and its Torah, while of great value, were dispensable. His views were unpopular, until the destruction of the temple made them useful for understanding what faith in Jesus Christ meant in a post-temple world. When we read the New Testament, we do not see how important the temple was for early Christians, except perhaps in some passages in Luke and Acts. This is because the New Testament was written or selected entirely after the fall of the temple by leaders in the church and their successors who prevailed because over the long years after 70 C.E. a new understanding of both the Scriptures and Jesus Christ was required.

During the second and third centuries, the leaders of the church were bishops in the increasingly wealthy churches of the great urban centers of the eastern Roman Empire, as well as Rome itself. The writings they endorsed as Scripture were those documents that stressed submission, obedience, patience, and endurance. There were many rivals to the power and authority of these leaders, and these rivals endorsed different types of writings. Some stressed the ongoing work of the Spirit as embodied in their rival authority; some stressed the futility of taking this world seriously at all; others stressed the complete break with the Judean, increasingly Jewish, heritage of the church. The winning faction in these church struggles of the first three centuries was confirmed in its power when the Roman emperor, Constantine, adopted their organization and cult as his own early in the fourth century. The Scriptures authorized by this faction therefore became the New Testament. Thereafter the history of the New Testament is chiefly the history of its Roman rule. The history of the church's interpretation of Scripture is tumultuous and fractious, but no more so than the history of the formation of Scripture itself.

Unfortunately for those looking for absolute certainty and security in the Bible, the biblical canon does not fix the Word of God. All the canon does is define, in a potentially deceptive manner, a literary basis for the church's ongoing struggle (as James Sanders has put it) to interpret who we are and what we are called to do. Interpretation in the midst of the struggle to find the truth is the name of the game. Interpretation began with the writing process and continues in the reading process. Whether there are interpretive axioms to which all should assent is the question, not the answer, and the only way to find an answer is to enter the interpretive fray with energy, compassion, intelligence, prayer, and love. The canon is only a way station on the church's journey of almost three thousand years from David to us.

Part 3

THE BIBLE
TODAY

14.

Those "Bible-Denying Skeptics"

Millions view the Bible as a book from on high; they presuppose that it had a divine origin. They assume God *revealed* Scripture to those who wrote it. In this view the Bible is a seamless garment, God's word to humanity.

People who see the Bible in this way generally think of revelation as coming to humanity in two forms: general revelation, and special revelation. General revelation refers to what God reveals through the universe that is our home. In this view, we understand something of God by looking at the created order. Those who hold this view would also say that this general revelation is available to anyone who cares to examine it, not just to Christians; hence people in remote parts of the earth could, at least theoretically or in a general sense, know God. Some adherents of this view would even go so far as to concede that in some measure there is truth in all religions. However, they would also stress the importance of what they call special revelation. This refers to a specific revelation made by God personally. God "speaks," as it were, and humans write down what God says. It is this kind of revelation—God speaking—that is claimed for the Bible. It is assumed that it was written completely outside of a specific social context and is therefore of equal value for all time and all places.

Many who have become familiar with the differences in Scripture still hold the belief that in the Bible God speaks in a unique way, though they accept that revelation does not include the words. Realizing that the idea that the Bible was dictated by God cannot be sustained, they see God as revealing content and allowing the biblical authors to express this content in their own words. In this view the Bible is affected by the culture of the times in which its various books were written; nevertheless, it is a God-given revelation.

For those who assume the Bible has a divine origin, everything we have presented so far in this book about how the Bible was first begun and how it was eventually put together is of little consequence. For such people the historical facts of the Bible's authorship are overshadowed by their belief that the Bible is God's revelation to humanity, and in the end of the day that is all that matters to them.

It is our contention that *what is meant by revelation must be determined in light of how the Bible actually came into being.* The Bible is, as we have seen, a cultural product. But acknowledging this truth does not exclude revelation. In our view there is no division between general and special revelation. Rather than falling into distinctly different categories, revelation exists on a continuum. God's word was not "dropped down out of the sky" at some point in the past but is present at all times. Some are more open to perceive it than others. Certain cultural conditions, prevalent at particular moments and in particular places in history, facilitate a greater understanding of what God is revealing than do conditions at other times.

The prospect of viewing the Bible this way understandably makes many people anxious. It means finding the Bible less simple than before. It means learning quite a lot that we did not know before. It means facing uncertainty about what such Bible study might lead to. Things previously believed might turn out to be different. Then what? What will we be left with to hold on to? Difficult as these questions are, faith calls us to have the courage to tackle them honestly instead of shying away from them.

Can Millions of People Be Wrong?

Millions of people accept the Bible as a divinely inspired book, treating it as if it were an entity, the Word of God, without ever questioning this idea. They never ask *Why do I believe this?* They believe it simply because they have always heard that it is the case.

Sometimes widely held beliefs turn out to be myths. We presuppose something to be the case because everyone says it is so, but we have never examined it.

A modern case of a popular myth is a classic example. It demonstrates that though millions may believe something, it is not necessarily the case. If ever there was a symbol of modern American culture, it is McDonald's. But what few know is that the story of how the fast-food restaurant chain was founded is a myth. McDonald's celebrates Founder's Day each year in honor of "founder Ray Kroc," who died in 1984, even though two brothers, Maurice and Richard McDonald, originated the concept of fast-food, opened America's first fast-food restaurant in San Bernardino, California, in 1948, introduced the famous golden arches, and had opened nine McDonald's restaurants and sold twenty-one franchises before they hired Kroc as a franchise agent in 1955. Kroc formed a franchising company of his own, however, and in 1960 changed its named to McDonald's Corporation. By 1961, when the McDonald brothers sold out to Kroc, the Corporation had spawned over 200 McDonald's restaurants.

The myth that Kroc was the founder began with his autobiography in 1977. There he states that he founded the chain and built it up starting with his first restaurant in Des Plaines, Illinois. Kroc was more ambitious than the McDonalds and was the force behind what became the billion-dollar, culture-changing hamburger restaurant chain familiar to everyone the world over. But the idea that he alone was the "founder" means forgetting all history before 1955, if not 1961. Richard McDonald is today still alive and happy in his split-level home in Manchester, New Hampshire, though occasionally bitter about the oblivion that Kroc has cast over his role in the early years of McDonald's.

Another example of a cherished myth of modern American society is the question of who invented baseball. The myth that baseball was invented by Abner Doubleday, later a Civil War hero, in Cooperstown, New York, in 1839 was formulated in a report published on December 30, 1907, by a commission headed by the baron of sporting goods, millionaire Albert Spalding. The game, he wrote, "is the exponent of American Courage, Confidence, Combativeness; American Dash, Discipline, Determination; American Energy, Eagerness, Enthusiasm." Today most Americans are aware of the myth but not the truth about the origin of baseball—even though the truth, including how the myth got started, is, in addition to being true, much more interesting.

Baseball in fact developed out of the British children's game called rounders, which one can see being played on playgrounds all over Britain today. An American named Alexander Joy Cartwright turned rounders into baseball by laying down three bases ninety feet apart, locating the batter at home plate, setting the number of players on a side at nine, deciding on nine innings, with each inning concluding with the third out rather than having all batters bat in each inning, among other changes. This is how what was originally the gentleman's game of baseball got started. Spalding, who invented the myth, had no use for the idea that all-American baseball had evolved out of English child's play. Spalding's view prevailed, as in 1939 the supposed centennial of the invention of baseball was celebrated all over the United States and the Baseball Hall of Fame was founded in Cooperstown.

When people who are used to believing the Bible to be of divine origin hear that certain scholars do not believe Adam and Eve were real people, that they deny the historicity of Noah's Flood, that they doubt the biblical claim that the walls of Jericho fell down, or that they do not believe that the exodus actually happened, these people tend to dismiss such scholars with a statement such as, "Oh, he's one of those Bible-denying skeptics." Scholars who question the Bible are portrayed as trying to tear down the authority of the Bible.

Far from wanting to tear down the authority of the Bible, biblical scholars take a questioning approach to the Bible in order better to hear and understand what the Bible has to say. When popular assumptions prevail over historical realities, much of the richness of Scripture is lost from view. When it is seen in relation to what is now known about ancient peoples, events, and languages, what the Bible is saying to us is clarified and enhanced many times over.

Only a few decades ago little was known about the world of the Bible. But in recent years a vast amount of historical information has become available to anyone who takes the trouble to find out about it. It is this wealth of knowledge, particularly from archaeology, that has led scholars to reconsider earlier ways of understanding the Bible.

To read the Bible in the light of history is to approach the Bible and the faith it nourishes with integrity, giving due consideration to what archaeologists, linguists, and historians have discovered.

A questioning approach to Scripture — an approach that utilizes the tools of historical inquiry to examine the Bible in the search for truth, rather than merely seeking to defend cherished beliefs — can help us cut through myth-making and unlock meanings which in turn lead us to a richer, deeper, more realistically based faith.

Getting at the Truth

Historical inquiry tends to dispel misperceptions and misunderstandings. An example of how it can help us gain a more accurate, realistic picture concerns the man famed for the discovery of America, Christopher Columbus. While the memory of Columbus is venerated in classrooms across Europe and throughout the North American continent, the story of how "in 1492 Columbus sailed the ocean blue" is viewed somewhat differently by most of the people of the Americas outside the United States, who regard Columbus as an ambiguous figure if not an outright scoundrel. Given the oppression that resulted from Spanish and Portuguese conquests in the Americas, the widespread misgivings about Columbus are not surprising.

Open inquiry based on methodological doubt, painstaking examination of available evidence, comparison with plausible generalizations, attention to context, and ongoing challenges from alternative views call into question the view that Columbus' conquests are to be celebrated unambiguously. When we look more closely at the standard picture of Columbus, we no longer see the noble sailor setting out in search of geographical truth and discovering America. Instead we see a man who, though undeniably courageous, was also an endlessly avaricious, opportunistic merchant who reflected the cultural assumptions of his contemporaries in his vicious, cynical cruelty toward literally scores of thousands of native inhabitants of the lands he conquered.

Not only is Columbus as a great discoverer a partial, and therefore distorted, picture of reality, but it turns out that Columbus' famous struggle against the ignorance and rigidity of people who insisted the earth was flat is also a bit of a red herring. In Columbus' day, nearly everyone knew the earth was round. The real threat to ignorance came not long after Columbus, when Copernicus reasoned that the sun rather than the earth was at the center of the world. This view was published in 1543, and was confirmed through mathematical calculations by Kepler (1571-1630) and through observations by Galileo (1564-1642). This development signaled the beginnings of the spread of inquiry into all areas of human life in the seventeenth and eighteenth centuries.

The Birth of Widespread Skepticism

The church tried to suppress the views of Copernicus and Galileo but failed. The reason it failed, and the reason the church since then has failed to suppress other developments in reasoned inquiry, is not some new popularity of science as opposed to religion. It has to do with our sense of what we call secular society and culture—with how we define what is "religious."

It was in the seventeenth century, in the time between Galileo and Newton, that the scientific revolution that led to the modern world got underway. Before then the world was viewed very differently from how we view it today. The universe comprised three tiers. Beneath the earth was the underworld, while above it stretched a dome on which the sun, moon, and stars revolved. God dwelled beyond the dome, and from this lofty position God ruled the world. The hierarchies that governed nations were decreed by God, so that everyone had a fixed role – lords and servants, rich and poor. God ordained that things be the way they are. When natural disasters occurred, people thought God was punishing them for something they had done wrong. Whenever things went wrong in life, it was God's doing. The question in people's minds was not how things happened, but why. What have we done to bring such punishment upon ourselves? This was a world of superstition in which demons and goblins lurked behind every lamp post and under every bed.

But around four centuries ago a fundamental change took place in how we understand the world. The secular was severed from the religious. Indeed today we often think of what is secular as opposed to what is religious. The secular includes everything that is not "religious" and is potentially the enemy of religion.

And yet, the basis of our notion of what is secular and why it seems to be not religious is not really tied up with science or history but with something even more pervasive and practical, our notions of government and law. In the United States we are heirs of views of government and law which developed especially during the seventeenth century. The idea that institutions of government and law could function separately from the church had developed already in the High Middle Ages, during the twelfth century. But it took many centuries for this idea to become widely established, to receive clear articulation and rationale, and to influence the many other aspects of society and culture. This happened in large part due to the Protestant Reformation itself, not least through Protestant notions of the separate realms of church and state.

In their separate but related ways, Grotius, Hobbes, and Locke – all belonging to the seventeenth century – developed theories of society that entailed humans themselves taking responsibility for ordering their lives through government. This was radically different from the earlier world view in which God ran the show. When such theories became embodied in the political institutions and revolutions of the eighteenth century, including the American Revolution, the idea that a valid and important arena of life existed apart from the authority of the church was here to stay. For instance, for the first time in modern history it became tenable that not just God could make and unmake marriages but the state also.

The Bible Comes under Scrutiny

It was under these circumstances that historical inquiry into the Bible began. This is why historical inquiry into matters of faith is seen by many as secular and not religious. Ironically, our sense of political freedom is directly related to our sense of the secular realm as distinct from the religious realm. We may value the one and feel hesitant about the other. But in fact this historical perspective reminds us that the supposedly religious and secular are inextricably tied up with each other even today, and that our sense of the religious, which is very different from what people would have thought was religious before the seventeenth century, is a result of our own social and cultural conditioning.

An even greater threat to the authority of established churches and customs came later, with the publication of Darwin's *Origin of the Species* in 1859, in which the methods of historical inquiry were applied to the question of the origin of the diversity of living things. Darwin's book aroused a great deal of resistance when it appeared, and the turmoil surrounding its implications for Christian faith has not died down yet.

It is hard for many today to put themselves back a mere hundred and fifty years, when practically no one was aware that the world was any older than the six thousand years or so implied by the Bible's chronology. Within a few decades it was clear that far from being a few thousand years old, the world was billions of years old. This fundamentally contradicted not just the first chapter of the Bible but people's sense of the framework of historical time that had previously been provided by the Bible. At the same time, archaeology was opening up an entire ancient world, previously completely unknown, which lasted for thousands of years, in which the Bible came quite late. Fundamentalism as we know it arose in the nineteenth and early twentieth centuries precisely as a reaction against such developments. It is not simply the way everybody always thought about the Bible.

While much in our cultural surroundings may suggest that reading the Bible as a work shaped by the forces of history is unchristian, to read the Bible with a questioning mind is in reality only to do today what courageous Christians have done for the last two thousand years for the greater vitality of the church. In fact the practice of reexamining the assumptions on which one's faith is built finds its roots in the Old Testament prophets, and in Jesus and Paul. They all looked long and hard at supposed truths of their time and found many of them questionable. Despite being bitterly opposed by people who did not like the tradition subjected to scrutiny, they continued to question, reconsider, and reformulate their beliefs. It was out of just such a reconsideration of Scriptural faith that the Christian church was born.

Does it not, then, behoove us to continue in the questioning tradition that has always been the hallmark of true faith? How else can we hope to hear the Word of God concerning the great issues of our time?

15.

What Do We Mean . . .

"Inspiration"?

Many of the religious leaders of Jesus' time made the mistake of honoring Scripture while failing to recognize that God is still actively engaged in the process of self-revelation. "You search the scriptures, because you think that in them you have eternal life," said Jesus, "yet you refuse to come to me that you may have life" (Jn 5:39-40). Important as the Bible is to us, like many two thousand years ago we can fossilize faith by refusing to believe that God is still speaking to us today.

The Bible is of inestimable value to our faith, but it is nevertheless still only a witness to the living faith that Christ inspires in the community of faith. It must therefore be read with a questioning mind, not with superficial and naive assent. We must enter into responsible dialogue with how our fathers and mothers in times past conceived of God as recorded in Scripture, but we cannot simply duplicate their finite understanding for our time. The book must not replace Christ as the head of the church; it must not become our god. Catholics have always understood this, and in recent decades several of the larger Protestant bodies have become increasingly aware of the danger of fossilizing the Word of God in Scripture.

A case in point is the Presbyterians. In good Reformed fashion, the Westminster Confession, which was written a hundred years after the Reformation and did not become the basis of Presbyterian teaching for another fifty years after that, placed the doctrine of Scripture at the beginning of its scheme, and took the trouble to list the books of the Bible so there would be no doubt what was in Scripture. This was a good example of the Reformation claim that the Bible forms the basis of faith and practice, a claim that severed the Reformed churches in their struggle to differentiate themselves from the powerful Roman Catholic church of their time.

Yet Presbyterians in the twentieth century voted overwhelmingly to supplement or supersede the understanding of faith implied by the organization of the Westminster Confession. The Confession of 1967, an official part of the Constitution of the Presbyterian Church (U.S.A.), places its teaching on the Bible within the section on the Holy Spirit, while the basis of confession is expressed instead in the person and work of Jesus Christ, to whom the Bible bears witness. The bedrock of the Word of God is Jesus Christ. Thus the Confession of 1967 acknowledges that the Bible does not speak for itself but must be interpreted, and that the interpretation of the Bible depends, as people in both the Reformed and Catholic churches have always held, on the witness of the Spirit working in and through the communion of the church itself. The meaning of the Bible comes from people in the church reading the Bible, by the guidance of the living Spirit embodied in the church.

When we base our ideas on a particular interpretation of the Bible, we find there are a thousand and one interpretations. So no matter how outlandish a televangelist's teachings may be, there's always someone who will subscribe to them. But when the Christ through the Spirit leads our lives, and the book becomes a tool to point us to our Creator instead of functioning as a "paper pope," we are freed up to enter into meaningful dialogue not only with Scripture but with the whole church. We're no longer interested in defending a pet point of view but in submitting ourselves to truth no matter what its source.

When faith is vitally alive, the church becomes a community of loving human beings who model the new humanity that Jesus represented. We cease saddling people with our personal hang-ups and allow them to chart their own spiritual journey within the community of faith. We foster a desire for truth, a spirit of inquiry, in an atmosphere of acceptance and love. We are well aware that the letter, as the apostle Paul called it, condemns and deadens our inner being; only the spirit can give life.

In the 1960s the hit movie *Those Magnificent Men in Their Flying Machines* fictionalized the early days of flying. A newspaper magnate sponsored an air race across the English channel, something that had never been done before. To win was a matter of national prestige, and countries all around the world sent flying machines to enter the race. On the day of the race, the German pilot gets the runs and cannot fly. His chief officer, who has never flown, has to substitute. When he is asked how he will fly the machine, he replies, "In the same way a German officer does everything—by the book!" First instruction: sit down! Needless to say, he ditches in the English Channel. Too many Christians are ditching in the chaos of life because they read the Bible in a naive, literalist fashion, as if the book were an instruction manual, instead of allowing themselves to be moved by the same Spirit that inspired the biblical authors and peoples.

A Living Faith

An alive faith has a salvation—a wholeness—to offer our broken and fragmented world. It can bring us the justice and equality, founded in the love, joy, and peace of the Spirit, that Jesus brought the people of his day. It can heal our fractured personhood.

Jesus' individual life is unrepeatable. It was a specific response to a given historical situation, a situation that will never be duplicated. If we are to follow Jesus today, it is no use asking the popular question, "What would Jesus have done?" More appropriate is the question, "What should we do, led by the Spirit of Christ?" The Spirit of Christ will guide us to a response to our historical situation that is appropriate for our own place in history. When faith is vitally alive, we will not retrace the path Jesus followed over nineteen hundred years ago; instead, our faith will lead us to recreate that path in a manner fitting for our own time and culture. To follow Jesus does not mean we live as he lived as a Judean in the first century. It is not a question of going back to see what answers he gave to problems in his own time, or what course of ethical or moral action he prescribed for people in Roman-occupied Palestine. It is a matter of discovering Jesus' attitude and allowing the living Christ to inspire that attitude in us today. To live in the Spirit is to learn how to live not Jesus' life centuries ago, but our own today.

Paul wrote to the Philippians, "Work out your own salvation" (2:12). Not work *for* salvation, which we then get as a reward when we die, but *work out.* Salvation is something we have to work out for ourselves in everyday life, just as we have to work out a relationship or a business deal. Then Paul adds, "For God is at work in you." It is God who impels us to become whole people, which is what salvation is. God is the one who generates the new life in us, modeled after the life of Jesus of Nazareth without being a replica of his life.

Salvation is not a gift God gives us like a present wrapped up nicely in a package so we can put it in front of the Christmas tree and gaze at it. It is not something we save and open only when we die. It is a life. It is to live with a certain attitude, a certain frame of mind, a certain quality of life. It is to experience the Christ's input into our lives on an everyday basis, transforming us into a more fully human, more lovely, more worthwhile individual, and uniting us together in a community of openness, honesty, acceptance, and love known as the body of Christ. When such a community is created, the Christ is present in the church.

The Bible: An Indispensable Instrument

Then what place do we give the Bible in the Christian tradition? As agents of God's new humanity, the Bible will be for us a resource book but not a rule book. The difference can be seen by contrasting what Lenin bequeathed to the Russian people with what the framers of the Constitution bequeathed to the people of the United States.*

*The authors are grateful to the writer of a letter published in the Presbyterian leadership magazine *Monday Morning* for the following illustration.

In a tomb in Moscow lies the mummified body of Vladimir Lenin. Through the miracle of the mortician, Lenin received a blessing expected of saints: Russia canonized its first Communist leader. Because the Russians idolized Lenin, it was for a long time extremely difficult for the USSR to change with the times and adopt appropriate approaches to current problems. Although Communism over the decades moderated from the extreme revolutionary stance of the founding fathers, the mummified, canonized leader of yesteryear long continued to exert a powerful influence on the people.

As a mummified Lenin reinforced the belief that the Russian regime is the summit of human genius, so at the time of the celebration of the 200th anniversary of the signing of the Constitution, Americans were being directed back to the framers of the Constitution. These framers did not have their mummies put on display in Constitution Hall, there to exert their influence for all time to come. They are not on display for us to reminisce, "See them here, stuffed, waxed, smiling in agreement."

Often idealized as men of high religious principle, with vision and a passion for justice, the framers of the Constitution were in truth anything but single-minded. Some were passionate, others almost unfeeling. Some were visionary, others notoriously pessimistic. Some were devoutly religious, others devoutly opposed to religion. They were men of contradictory interests and viewpoints, a skeptical and divided lot with no single opinion to which we might return for security in this age. More often than not they agreed most deeply on those measures in the Constitution that would counter the powers of the others.

The Constitution of the United States did not descend from heaven. It was hammered out in the contemporary world of the framers to address their specific problems. It did not anticipate a world revolutionized by technology. Nor was it the intent of the framers that it should do so. Rather than being the be-all-and-end-all of everything, it was intended to furnish us with a common basis for ongoing discussion of issues central to the American way of life. The framers sought to provide us with a framework within which to share our ideas, not a "thus saith the Lord."

What the framers gave us was a Constitution that ensures

everyone gets in on the discussion, even as they did, with their many different opinions. It was intended not to dictate our future but to guarantee that no one individual or group ever dictates our future. Freedom to discuss and hammer out our own answers to issues in a manner appropriate to our own time was the framers' intent. The Constitution, with its branches of government and counterbalancing of powers and amazing flexibility, with its built-in adaptability and need for revision, was meant to serve not as a dictator but as a safeguard against any form of dictatorship. That is why its framers, unlike Lenin, do not lie in open view. Though remembered for their work, they are buried with the past. They gave us a basis on which to talk to each other, and it is up to us, the living, to continue that talk as befits the needs of our own time.

The Meaning of Inspiration

There is a parallel between how the Constitution and the Bible came into being. We have seen that it is a fantasy that the various books of the Bible descended from heaven as perfect documents composed by God and communicated in writing by individual authors who wrote without error. The Bible records the process of a people of faith in history trying to discern the presence of God in their history—a God both immanent and transcendent, constantly beckoning them toward the horizons. Even as the Constitution was the product of a community with diverse opinions and practices revolving around a common goal, so too are the books of the Bible the product of a believing community in which traditions were developed, handed down, criticized, refined, altered to fit new conditions, and added to by newer insights and interpretations, just as has been done with the Constitution.

We can draw a further parallel between the Constitution and the Bible in terms of inspiration. The Constitution may be said to be inspired by the spirit of the American people. By "inspired" we do not mean that the American people dictated its wording, but that those who wrote it accurately reflected concerns of the American people and addressed issues that are relevant to America as a nation. Its framers were inspired by us insofar as they raised the questions that are in all our minds.

The biblical books may be said to be inspired in a similar way. Though they endorse theories about life and the universe that were current when the various books were written, and that we now know to be invalid; though their knowledge of scientific and historical data was limited and often plain wrong; though their understanding of human beings and why they are the way they are and do the things they do lacks the refinement and accuracy afforded by modern psychology; though they exclude people and points of view as churches often do today, they nevertheless breathe with the life of God, for they address those issues of human life with which God is most concerned. Inspiration means that as the biblical writers reflected on life in relationship to the dimension of the divine, they captured something of God's purpose for the world. The authors repeatedly raised the right questions. The inspiration is in the struggle to understand and be guided, not in the tablets on which the struggle was recorded.

The books of the Bible are literary attempts to express the inexpressible in human terms. Their stories are often not factual reporting of conversations and actions that took place, but more like legend. But that there is a legendary dimension to them does not mean the stories are void of value. Indeed the stories are packed with meaning for our everyday lives. They raise the issues that concern us all and that are of particular importance for God in dealing with the world. That is why we may rightly speak of them as inspired. They were composed not to "wow" us with the supernatural, but to introduce us to the God of miracle who is at work in our midst through the ordinary events of life.

Throwing the Baby out with the Bath Water

To argue as some do that if one statement in the Bible is inaccurate then we cannot trust any of it is completely misleading. It is a case of throwing the baby out with the bath water. That a literary work is not totally accurate does not invalidate the work. If we were to pick up a historical novel set in the

South at the time of the Civil War, we would find both fact and legend present. Some of the places, people, and events would have the ring of factuality. Other elements of the story would clearly be fictional. But whether factual or fictional, the story as a whole would have a ring of authenticity. It would enable us to enter into the world of the South in Civil War days and understand what was taking place in the society of that time.

How would we know what is factual? In one sense it would not matter. To get the point would be the important thing. But if we wish to concern ourselves with factuality, we have only to turn to the historians and archaeologists for answers. If the novel described a battle at Harrisonburg in central Louisiana we would know that to be factual. But if it described a small, modern, agricultural town in central Louisiana as a city of fifty thousand, with a large military fort that was headquarters for the Confederate forces in this region, archaeologists would quickly reject that as legend. Nevertheless the description of life in this small town, and particularly of activities surrounding the fort, might well give us an accurate picture of life in a fortified city in Civil War days.

Many of the biblical books are a lot like historical novels. It is the task of historians, archaeologists, and other biblical scholars to sort out fact from fiction; it is our task to understand the great truths to which the stories point, whether fact or fiction, and to be transformed by them. As Jesus expressed it, if anyone does what he taught, he or she will know whether or not the teaching is inspired. The proof of the pudding is in the eating.

Again and again Jesus steered the people of his time away from rigid interpretations that would literalize Scripture, as if the written word were the be-all-and-end-all of everything. They were to judge not by appearances—not at a simplistic, surface level—but to go deep and make an accurate assessment of an issue. That necessitated entering into dialogue with Scripture. Moses was not to be accepted as a final authority but to be questioned, debated, reasoned with. Again and again Jesus and the early church decided issues differently from Moses.

Jesus didn't leave us a book, a manual that answers every question. He left us a living community with a tradition that was passed on through that community, debated by that community, modified by that community, and added to by that community. It has always been the community that has written the Scriptures. The New Testament writings arose out of the questions and debates that were current in the early church, each being penned to address a real issue of the day, just as the Old Testament arose out of the struggles of the nation of Israel.

Even as the early New Testament community disagreed with and changed rulings that had been sacred to the people of God for thousands of years, so do we today. Circumcision was the lynch pin of the whole of the law of Moses including the Ten Commandments, but the church through long and agonizing debate arrived at the conclusion that it was no longer necessary. "For neither circumcision counts for anything nor uncircumcision," Paul decided (I Cor 7:19). What counts is becoming a new creation. In line with this emphasis on the new creation, in which there is neither male nor female, bond nor free, more and more Protestant churches today ordain women as well as men, and many ordain the divorced.

"Peace and mercy be upon all who walk by this rule," Paul added. The Greek word translated "rule" is the same word we use when we speak of the canon of the Bible. It means a measuring stick, a ruler. Moving toward becoming a new creation, a new humanity in which love, joy, peace, patience, kindness, goodness, faithfulness, gentleness, and self-control rule us is our only law today. All these qualities relate to our dealings with others. What counts isn't whether we observe this day or that day, engage in this ritual or that ritual, hold to this moral code or that moral code. What counts is whether as participants in the body of Christ we value ourselves and everyone else as daughters and sons of the Creator, whether we love and accept people just as they are as did Jesus, and whether we seek to serve and help others instead of taking advantage of them and misusing them.

The community of Christ formulates its own lifestyle, then, in conversation with the written record left by its first proponents, in response to the Spirit, and in ongoing discussion between all of its constituent parts. As with the U. S. Constitution, it moves forward through a system of checks and balances, guided by the living Christ, present in the church wherever his revolutionary Spirit is welcomed.

16.

How To Use the Bible Today

What we have been uncovering about the Bible will be shocking to many. More than one person's faith has been shaken upon discovering that the biblical record cannot be read literally or regarded as factual. The question that immediately springs to most minds is, "If parts of the Bible are not factual, what is factual? Can I trust anything in the Bible?"

For instance, we have seen that there are two entirely different creation stories at the beginning of Genesis. We have learned the meaning of creation stories. Since they are not about how the world actually came into being, what are we to make of the so-called Fall that people are used to associating with the Garden of Eden story? Was there never a Fall? Could it be that science is right, that there never was a perfect creation but rather an evolving universe, albeit an evolution inspired by the Creator? And what then of our understanding of human nature and of how the human race got into its present predicament in terms of all the injustice in the world? Is this the remnants of an evolving animal nature, to which has been added the spiritual capacity of the more recently developed cerebral cortex? What, also, of the concept of sexuality and marriage spelled out in the garden story? Is it still meaningful for us today? How are we to understand these stories in terms of modern life?

An Emerging Picture

It is the claim of the New Testament that in the person of Jesus of Nazareth the reign of God was inaugurated. The end of the old world order was sealed at Calvary, and at Easter the world entered the last days of the old order as a new age began to dawn. The mighty tide of history began flowing in a new direction. Bit by bit the social pyramid that has enabled the few to exercise autonomy in their lives while the masses are oppressed is being inverted, and in recent centuries we have seen giant steps toward freedom and equality in the West, and now also in the East.

Jesus in parables spoke of the reign of God in terms of a leavening agent mixed into flour. Silently, almost imperceptibly, the yeast goes to work until the whole mixture is transformed. He spoke of God's reign as a tiny mustard seed that grows and grows until it becomes the largest of herbs, a veritable bush that provides shelter and protection.

During this long period of gestation, as we await the birthing of a humanity in which all are valued, all are treated with equal love and justice, we who are allied with God in this task of ushering in the new world find ourselves living in an overlap of two different worlds. The old is perishing though still very much around us; the new is sprouting up but not yet in bloom. God's reign is emerging in society, but fragmentarily, here and there, a little at a time. And that means that we are affected not only by the character of the new world but also by the false values and dehumanizing ways of the old.

So it was that, after living with them day and night, Jesus said to his disciples on the eve of his arrest, "I have yet many things to say to you, but you cannot bear them now" (Jn 16:12). The folk who followed Jesus were culturally conditioned. They belonged to a society whose norms and traditions were far from God's intention for humanity. Jesus was able to show his follow-ers some aspects of what the new creation he was inaugurating would look like, but there were many things they were just not ready to hear. Their culture, their place in history, simply did not permit them to hear.

At its inception the church did not have the full picture of what God's reign would look like, not even most of the picture. Rather, in Jesus' own words, there was much yet to be revealed. Indeed what the world to come would look like was hidden from them, for Jesus went on to say, "When the Spirit of truth comes, it will guide you into all the truth ... and it will declare to you the things that are to come." Jesus had outlined the new world in broad terms; but had he told them what the skeleton he had sketched would look like when fully fleshed out, it would have shocked them because it stands so much of their culture on its head.

The New Testament shows how, just as Jesus promised, the Spirit early on began weaning the church from a culture promoted by the Hebrew Scriptures. They quickly learned that simply because it was "what the Bible says" did not necessarily mean it was to be continued in the new age. It may no longer be "true" for the life of the individual believer or for the believing community. On issue after issue, as the Spirit brought to bear upon them the values of the new world, the church found themselves acting contrary to specific "thus saith the Lord" of the only Bible the church at that time knew.

When Paul Got It Wrong

One reason we can trust the New Testament's record of the development of the church is that it preserves not only the apostles' successes but also how they got it wrong on many issues and had to unlearn much of what they grew up believing. For instance, for several years they thought that the Good News was only for Judeans. Certainly the Old Testament was plain enough in its statements that the world would be converted to Judean religion when the Messiah came. So it appalled nearly everybody when the Spirit led Peter into a Roman soldier's house and made believers of Gentiles without first requiring that they begin observing the Judean law as set forth in Scripture. The apostles in Jerusalem called him on the carpet for it. And later when Paul taught people throughout the Empire that they didn't have to be circumcised, didn't have to observe the Sabbath, and could eat pork and shell fish, that was too much even for Peter, who ended up in a major conflict with Paul and had to be set straight.

Paul certainly changed with regard to many Old Testament practices, but he recognized that the church still had much to learn beyond what he could presently see. Indeed if we imagine

Paul was free of cultural biases, personal opinions, and error, we contradict Paul himself. "As for prophecies, they will pass away," he wrote; "as for tongues, they will cease; as for knowledge, it will pass away" (I Cor 13:8). Paul realized that what had seemed appropriate for one period of history, what had seemed helpful, what had seemed clear, would be found inadequate as greater understanding of the new order emerged. He continued, "For our knowledge is imperfect and our prophecy is imperfect; but when the perfect comes, the imperfect will pass away." Yes, Paul, who wrote those wonderful letters that make up much of our New Testament, got it wrong at times (though he probably didn't like to admit it).

If a problem arose in a congregation Paul had planted, they wrote to him for advice. How did Paul handle such a situation? Was he a repository of all knowledge, infallible? When a problem came up, he addressed it with all the insight God was able to show him given the limitations of his place in history. He gave it his best shot. Sometimes he called it right, and sometimes he called it wrong. To paraphrase him, "My understanding is somewhat hazy," he admitted; "I see some of the picture, but it's still pretty dim."

The New Testament records how Paul changed his mind on many issues as he grew. In his earlier writings he taught that when we die we are unconscious until the resurrection. Later writings express a quite different view. The church came to see that resurrection occurs at death, so that we are immediately with the Lord. In his earlier career Paul agreed with the Jerusalem apostles that Gentiles were not to eat meat butchered in sacrifice to a pagan deity. Later he taught Gentiles that idols couldn't jinx the meat, and if it didn't upset their conscience and wouldn't offend anyone, to eat such meat was fine. In his earlier writings he expected the end of the age imminently, with the bodily return of Jesus, and boldly proclaimed that he would live to see it. Later he realized that he was going to die and that God was involved in a lengthy process of world revolution that is far more complex than the simple return of Jesus. In fact Paul came to see the second coming of Christ in terms of the transformation of the cosmos (Rom 8:17-39).

Another issue Paul and his successors changed on concerned

widows. To the Corinthians Paul wrote that if a woman's husband dies, "she is free to be married to whom she wishes, only in the Lord. But in my judgment she is happier if she remains as she is. And I think that I have the Spirit of God" (I Cor 7:39-40). Paul felt inspired to tell widows to remain single. This led to the creation of a special order for widows, whose support was a benevolent responsibility of the church. That was all well and good if the end of history was imminent. But when the church realized Paul was wrong and history was nowhere near ending, they saw it was impossible to support a growing order of widows interminably. So when we read the much later letter to Timothy, we find that widows who were less than sixty years old were encouraged to remarry. "I will therefore that the younger women marry, bear children, guide the house," says the author (I Tim 5:14 KJV). That is a distinct change from Paul's earlier advice. The church's understanding of how the new world would come about had changed, and therefore the guidance changed.

Inspiration Not the Same as Infallibility

The apostles never claimed inerrancy or infallibility, only inspiration. It is common for people to substitute the words "inerrant" or "infallible," but "inspired" has no such overtones. When God inspired the prophets or apostles, God did not give them words or facts but put the facts known to them in the light of ultimate meaning and moved them to speak in the language they knew. Paul was inspired because what he wrote breathes with the life of God. His vision of what God is doing in history, and of the meaning of the church in the world, is a God-given vision. But infallible? Inerrant? Paul would have been appalled.

To be grasped by a vision does not mean we immediately see all of its ramifications for the workaday world. As Paul himself explained, "For now we see in a mirror dimly, but then face to face. Now I know in part; then I shall understand fully, even as I have been fully understood" (I Cor 13:12). Paul's knowledge of how the new order will look when it has come in full was partial, he admitted. His understanding was limited, he said. On some issues, he confessed, his insight was pretty dim.

For instance, although Paul at moments articulated a vision of there being no difference in the spiritual status of male and female in God's new age, what that really meant never dawned on him. He was the product of a patriarchal culture and therefore could not understand the full implications of the gospel in this regard.

In parts of the Old Testament, women are treated as inferior to men; indeed throughout much of Israel's history women were regarded as little more than chattels. The law itself regarded them this way.* Since he was schooled in the law and was a thoroughgoing product of a culture that for thousands of years had been dominated by males, it should not surprise us that some of Paul's statements in the New Testament continue this tradition of treating women as inferior to men.

Now, did the Spirit cease impacting human lives when the first apostles died? Or is Christ alive and still the active head of the church, still leading it through the Spirit? "I am with you to the end of the age," said Jesus. Those churches that react to the evolution of society around them as if evil were the dominant reality in the world, corrupting the church at every turn, evidently do not believe Jesus' promise. Because they operate out of a spirit of fearfulness, they fail to realize that God is sovereign on this planet, at work through the broad sweep of history to birth the new creation. They therefore cannot recognize the creating force behind the women's movement as the breath of God. Yes, there are excesses, because inspiration does not mean inerrancy. But the women's movement is inspired, in that it is moving humanity in the direction God means us to go. It has taken two thousand years for the Spiritual Presence to generate sufficient freedom in society for the Christ who is the head of the church to at last begin revealing to us the terrible sin of denying women the right to determine their own course in life and to use their talents to the full, whether in the home, the office, the Presidency, or the pulpit. The revelation has dawned upon parts of the church but not yet on the whole church.

When the Spirit blows, nothing ultimately can stand in its

*See *In the Beginning*, Robert B. Coote and David Robert Ord (Philadelphia: Fortress Press, 1992).

way. There is no turning back the revolution that has begun. God's new day is here and people who have been oppressed are coming into their own. We who are the revolutionary Christ's presence in society must push the revolution forward. We must stand against those who continue to oppress, demanding that pharaoh let God's people go. If we do not do so, the very stones will cry out.

The Bible and the Issues of Our Time

And now, new challenges face us.

Advances in medicine raise questions of ethical import never before faced by the church. To meet these challenges will require more than proof-texting from the Scriptures. At the same time we cannot ignore the Scriptures and the ways in which the church has interpreted them through the centuries. A relevant faith is not one that automatically accepts or applauds whatever new technological breakthrough is discovered. Answers must be hammered out carefully, painstakingly, responsibly through dialogue with the Scriptures, tradition, and the whole counsel of the church in its many modes of expression today.

Surrogate motherhood, made possible by the implanting of a fertilized egg, is one such issue. The last half of the twentieth century has witnessed a revolution in sexual ethics, again triggered by the advances of medical science. Safer, reliable forms of contraception, not to mention sterilization for both males and females, have altered society's attitudes toward sex. Since reproduction is no longer necessarily a consequence of sexual activity, marriage is now viewed by millions as only one form of legitimate sexual expression. The Bible will be an important tool in addressing such issues. While it does not answer our questions directly, it does furnish us with insight into what it means to be a human being and how we might promote our full humanity. These insights will inform our discernment as we tackle difficult ethical issues.

As churches struggle with what a Christian lifestyle looks like in a twentieth-century setting, people want to know what the

Bible says and whether what it says is true. We have seen that there are no easy answers. Proof-texting is not an answer. Experience teaches us that revelation doesn't come in the form of an unmistakable voice from heaven. God doesn't appear on television. Instead, insight into the infinite invades our intuition from the finite and the familiar. It is the natural world, with its ordinary, everyday events that is charged with the self-disclosure of the Creator.

Because revelation occurs in a concrete context it is always through a glass, darkly. We don't see face to face or know as we are known. We know only in part, so that all revelation is fragmentary. The limitations of our age and culture close us off from the beatific vision.

At a certain period in history a particular way of expressing an insight into the infinite may be meaningful, but if the mode of expression remains unchanged over a long period of time it may ultimately become hopelessly inadequate and therefore grossly misunderstood. It is not necessarily that the earlier expression did not convey truth; it is that the historical and cultural situation has changed so radically that what was meaningful in one epoch has become inappropriate for another.

If we are to have a vital faith, the formulations we use to express that faith must fit the world we live in and the growing understanding of God's purposes that the Creator's increasing self-revelation through history makes possible. As Jesuit Jon Sobrino has put it, we must find a different way to affirm what was said in the past precisely out of fidelity to the message of the past.

Before we can draw on a particular statement of Scripture to claim that it is "true" for us today, we must know a great deal about the text. Who wrote it, when, and why? What were the givens in the understanding of the writer, and do these align with the broad sweep of the biblical message of the value of all humans as individuals who bear the image of God? Biblical scholarship can guide us to informed answers to these questions.

If we are to know the truth and by it be set free, we must enter responsibly into dialogue with the wisdom of the ages, and glean from our fathers and mothers of the past insight to help guide us as we seek to be led by the Spirit in our modern era.

But we must enter into this dialogue with eyes and ears wide open and minds prepared, ready always to question preconceived notions, ready to modify and build on the insights of the past.

Suggested Reading

James Barr, *Beyond Fundamentalism: Biblical Foundations for Evangelical Christianity.* Philadelphia: Westminster Press, 1984; British title *Escaping from Fundamentalism*, London: SCM Press, 1984.

———, *Holy Scripture: Canon, Authority, Criticism.* Philadelphia: Westminster Press, and Oxford: OUP, 1983.

Phyllis A. Bird, *The Bible as the Church's Book.* Philadelphia: Westminster Press, 1982.

Frederick H. Borsch, ed., *The Bible's Authority in Today's Church.* Valley Forge: Trinity Press International, 1993.

Robert P. Carroll, *The Bible as a Problem for Christianity.* Philadelphia: Trinity Press International, 1991; British title *Wolf in the Sheepfold*, London: SPCK, 1991.

Gordon D. Fee and Douglas Stuart, *How to Read the Bible for All It's Worth: A Guide to Understanding the Bible.* Grand Rapids: Zondervan, 1981.

Robert M. Grant with David Tracy, *A Short History of the Interpretation of the Bible.* 2nd ed. Philadelphia: Fortress Press, and London: SCM Press, 1984.

John M. Hull, *What Prevents Christian Adults from Learning?* Philadelphia: Trinity Press International, 1991.

John Shelby Spong, *Rescuing the Bible from Fundamentalism: A Bishop Rethinks the Meaning of Scripture.* San Francisco: Harper San Francisco, 1991.

James D. Smart, *The Strange Silence of the Bible in the Church.* Philadelphia: Westminster Press, 1970 and London: SCM Press, 1971.

Krister Stendahl, *Meanings: The Bible as Document and as Guide.* Philadelphia: Fortress Press, 1984.